FEAR LESS,
SELL MORE

FIND YOUR COURAGE
and MAKE MILLIONS

TOM STERN

Post Hill
PRESS

A POST HILL PRESS BOOK

ISBN: 978-1-64293-882-1
ISBN (eBook): 978-1-64293-883-8

Fear Less, Sell More:
Find Your Courage and Make Millions
© 2021 by Tom Stern
All Rights Reserved

Post Hill Press, LLC
New York • Nashville
posthillpress.com

Published in the United States of America
1 2 3 4 5 6 7 8 9 10

Dedicated to the sweet memory of Noah Stern

CONTENTS

Section I: Fear Never Sleeps

Section II: How to Go from Fearful to Fear Less

Section III: Keep on Keeping On

I first met Tom Stern at a comedy club in New York City in the late '70s. Among the unknowns at that time were people like Jerry Seinfeld, Larry David, and Andy Kaufman. The first time I saw Tom perform, I knew immediately he would one day become a successful corporate recruiter and write a book called *Fear Less, Sell More*. Not to be cruel, but that's one of the harsh realities of show business—you need a combination of talent, luck, ambition, and have to be in the right place at the right time. Miss any one of these and it's over. The measure of a man is not if he wins or loses, but how he deals with the realities of his situation. Some turn to alcohol or drugs, or something worse. Others pick themselves up and play the hand they were dealt.

Tom pulled me aside one night and said, "Jay, I think I am better at selling ideas than writing them." That's the sort of honest self-assessment you rarely see in show business. I knew of an agency that was opening a West Coast office and thought Tom would be an excellent addition. Knowing comedians and comedy the way he did, he soon became head of the film and television department.

Oh, he's still doing shows—only now he does it one client at a time. Maybe he can teach you how to do it too.

—*Jay Leno*

Anytime you introduce an idea, two friends, or in this case, a book, it's tricky. You want to create anticipation for what is to follow while simultaneously building rapport and common ground. Establishing credibility is important, but puffery is alienating. It's a delicate balance. I remember one time I was nervous about a big speech and impressing the audience, so I wrote an introduction that referenced every accomplishment I'd ever achieved. Tone-deaf to how overblown it was, I asked my wife if there was anything I should add to the introduction and she said, "An intermission."

A poorly managed ego and its attendant expectations can create anxiety. Anxiety is definitely a double-edged sword. It can paralyze you, stagnating future possibilities, yet those same insecurities can fuel you to climb higher than you ever thought possible. Anxiety can be a curse or a blessing: you can be paralyzed by it, watching possibilities vanish, or fueled to climb higher than you ever thought possible. I've been both at different moments in my life and career.

Reflecting on my long journey with its bumpy lows and its exhilarating highs, I found the sales path in my late twenties was what organized my whole life and gave me an independence I never thought possible. I hadn't considered sharing that transformation and the lessons that led to it with other sales professionals until I hit an unanticipated milestone—arriving at my favorite movie theater to receive my first senior discount. I realized the time for legacy-building had come.

My story is odd in its contradictions. On the one hand, I was from a very affluent and powerful family, whose wealth and social standing had enabled extreme entitlement in me as a young man. (More than once I have said, "A carton of milk in the sun for a month would not have been as spoiled as I was.") Not a sympathetic portrait. Conversely, I had many challenges and difficulties, not of my own making, that paint a picture of isolation, neglect, and terrible insecurity. (In sharing my story, I recognize it is one of privilege, and it does not speak to the trying social and economic times we face today. However, its relevance is authenticity, which I believe is the foundation for all self-knowledge, a governing principle in my philosophy of attaining sales mastery.)

It seems both my life and career have intertwined two seemingly oppositional elements—confidence and fear. I spent my childhood intimidated by my family's legacy of success. My great-grandfather, Julius Rosenwald, took over Sears, Roebuck and Co. in its early years, making it a retail behemoth under his stewardship as CEO and chairman. He also pursued a highly impactful philanthropic mission—establishing a system of formal education for blacks in the South with the help of Booker T. Washington. My father, Alfred R. Stern, was outwardly charismatic but an emotionally distant man. One of the founders of cable television, the association's national chairman in the '60s, as well as the chairman of Mount Sinai Hospital, PBS, and other prestigious organizations, he ran our family as if it were a business. With its reviews and updates, the dinner table was more like a board meeting than a family gathering, thus his nickname "CEO

Dad." He only wanted to hear about achievement and success; intimacy and affection were not on the agenda. At the end of the meal, he would break down the discussion into a series of lessons and conclusions for the family moving forward, which is why I always said his favorite dessert was apple pie chart.

Of his three children, I was the most disappointing to him, with no visible talent besides making my mother and sister giggle at inopportune times, and my father was always overly critical of me. Each bad report card brought vehement condemnation. Would my CEO dad call me into his office one dark day and say, "Tom, I love you very much, but I'm going to have to let you go."? An absurd fantasy, but my emotional reality. This man I admired so much, whose love I so desperately sought, was out of reach. Sadly, my conclusion was as simple as it was devastating: I just wasn't good enough.

When each morning, I left our 4,000-square-foot upper East side pressure cooker for the Dalton School—one of Manhattan's most prestigious institutions of learning—things only got worse. There, my family's status could not protect me. An ADHD (attention deficit hyperactivity disorder) dyslexic with the nervous system of a gibbon, I had everything from physical tics to loud, rapid speech. It seemed I could not live up to the family name anywhere. I was unable to focus and listen, and it was clear the Dalton School was not equipped to educate me. In addition to my academic failures, my classmates would not accept me and took great pleasure in publicly mocking me. When I wasn't being humiliated, I was disruptive, and seemingly spent more time in the principal's office than in the classroom. Constantly getting in fights and bragging about my class-president-and-star-athlete-brother, Nicky, I had no friends and was desperately lonely. (I tried to joke it all away by telling my favorite teacher that even my imaginary friend wouldn't return my calls.)

I came home defeated every day, only to incur further judgment each night. My bedroom was my only sanctuary. It was there that I withdrew into a fantasy world, rocking on my bed for hours each night, imagining myriad ways I could succeed and show them all!

Careening toward the vast, deep space of my unconscious, whipsawed by grandiosity and a life devoid of self-esteem, I might have orbited a very empty and destructive place till my future had been extinguished. Fortunately, a candescent light pierced my dark despair. It emanated from my mother's smile every time I made her laugh. She seemed to intuitively sense that I was starved for support and gave it to me with the constant enthusiasm of a studio audience eagerly responding to a hyperactive applause sign. In her mind, there was nothing I couldn't do, and she constantly told me so.

She pushed me toward the arts: writing, singing, and acting. As I explored them all, she only cheered more loudly. Although I was still a melancholy and fragile individual, I found distraction and solace in these pursuits. I became the class clown to distract from my poor preparation. When my history teacher asked me if I knew who Caesar was, I replied, "He invented croutons." As I was thrown out of class, I could still hear the lingering laughs as I walked away, beaming. I believed all this performing would lead to fame and glory in entertainment, but looking back now, I realize those skills were actually training me to evolve into something I never considered or thought I wanted to be: a world-class salesman. Singing taught me to think of my speaking voice as an instrument, acting gave me a feel for the conscious intention and subtext behind conversations, and writing informed my understanding of the power of messaging through distinctive word choice.

After graduating college, the only business career I pursued was show business—specifically stand-up comedy. I came up the ranks with Jerry Seinfeld, Paul Reiser, and Bill Maher (then the MC at NYC's top comedy club, Catch a Rising Star. Bill often brought me on stage). It was thrilling hanging out with these future luminaries after the show at the Green Kitchen on First Avenue, devouring incredibly sugary cakes while trading jokes and stories. I always appreciated being in their company even as I stumbled home every night at two in the morning in a near diabetic coma.

Unfortunately for me, the party didn't last. These brilliant talents eclipsed me, rapidly moving up the ladder while I remained earthbound. As painful as the realization was that I couldn't compete with the best, I had learned so much from this singularly challenging art form. Reading a crowd's mood and sensibility was like combat training for communication strategies. Facing hostile and heckling audiences was an exercise in courage and improvisation that would help me overcome professional obstacles in the future.

I pursued writing and producing after moving to Los Angeles, and it was there that I began my sales career in pitch meetings. Selling ideas to Chris Ahlbrecht, the senior vice president of comedy at HBO and the company's future chairman, built my confidence. When none of my pitched projects made it to the little screen, once again I lost hope. It was here that Jay Leno saved me. I was running out of money and turned to him for help. A mentor to so many in comedy, he was always there to offer sage advice, often with gentle teasing. I had gotten to know Jay when I moved to LA and purchased my first car. Even then the resident expert on automobiles, he approved the stick-shift sports car I selected (thirty-plus years later, whether I talk to him on the phone or bump into him at Whole Foods, he always starts the conversation the same way: "So how's the Mazda?"). I met him at the Improv on Melrose in 1986. Despondent, I confided in him that I had lost faith in my writing skills. "No one ever produces my stuff. I think I'm better at selling ideas than I am at writing them." He offered to introduce me to Bob Williams, president of Spotlite Enterprises, the live-performance agency that represented him. "They're opening a West Coast office and are looking for a head of film and television."

I'm not 100 percent sure why they hired me; it may have been to please their number-one client, or because when Bob called me at seven in the morning two days later, I recognized his voice despite only three hours sleep and answered the phone as if I'd had three cups of coffee. They love the hint of infinite energy in showbiz.

I had finally become a full-time salesman. Daily lunches in Hollywood with producers, studio executives, and casting directors was fun. But the best part was getting the community excited about talent: Customizing each presentation for a very eclectic client base. Framing strengths, mitigating weaknesses, and seeing the *buy* look in their eye when I had them hooked. Whether I was on the set of a film, in the green room of *The Tonight Show*, or counseling a budding comedian in my office, I was always building relationships. I would have continued in that role for the rest of my career if the entertainment party culture hadn't drowned my brain in alcohol and marijuana.

Getting off the fast track and finding sobriety/recovery was the best thing I could have done. Leaving the industry, I found my way to executive recruiting by starting in the boiler room of a small firm, Princeton Corporate Consultants. Galvanized to raise a family and eager to stabilize my life, I had finally struck gold. The energy and passion I possessed for the art of sales consumed me, and I became Princeton's number-one producer four years' running. In 1994, the consulting arm of Price Waterhouse, my largest client, was looking at a giant expansion and offered me the chance of a lifetime. I started my own business, Stern Executive Search, and was their top external recruiter in North America for change integration.

Over the next six years, I placed more than 150 consultants with them at all levels and became a seven-figure earner. Along the way, I added clients like Deloitte, Ernst & Young, IBM, McKinsey, BCG, Bain, Sutherland Global Services, and many others. I rose to the top 5 percent of sole proprietors in the industry. A lot of it was luck, the tried-and-true cliché of being in the right place at the right time, but in deconstructing my career, my productivity also hinged on the skills I had garnered from my creative experiences. They were my foundation for selling success. After all, I didn't have an MBA or corporate sales training from a leading company. What I did have was the joy of applying creative instincts to a business process, specifically the art of influence and persuasion. Over the last thirty-one years, my career has become more than a pursuit of money or a transaction to be added to the ledger; it's an avenue to enjoy business relationships all over the world in a way that I had never been able to do with the kids in school or my workaholic father. (Ironically, as my success ascended, my father jumped on board with advice and encouragement—we finally found common ground and came full circle.)

I have shared meeting rooms with executives from the finest companies in the world. Harvard, Yale, and Princeton grads intimidated me the first few years. But this time, my childhood insecurities didn't defeat me. This time, my anxiety abated as I found resilience.

Rather than being swallowed up by fear, I focused on my senses, my imagination, my love of language, and saw every sales situation as an adventure, a performance where I could be my best self.

Not that it matters, but the following fable is inspired by a true story. So as you read, it should be clear that much of its substance has a direct corollary to my own experience. *Fear Less, Sell More* reflects my own gratitude; after a lifetime of struggling to overcome anxiety, I discovered a wellspring of joy in my career. It is my fervent hope that from this simple business tale, you will glean enough inspiration—even if some of the techniques do not resonate with you and not all the suggestions are bullseyes—and you will be energized by the growth and camaraderie of the characters. If I'm right and a pilot light is ignited in your spirit by this narrative, I am convinced that you will walk down the road to greater professional excellence with a little more spring in your step and the sense that it was there all along.

—*Tom Stern*
July 2020

SECTION I

FEAR NEVER SLEEPS

CHAPTER 1

WHY YOU NEED TO MANAGE SALES ANXIETY

M eet Chris. Like many salespeople, Chris is successful, not-so-successful, and everywhere in between, and wakes up each morning with a constant companion— the first voice Chris hears every morning:

Good morning, Chris. The sun is shining and it's going to be another terrifying day! Are we going to close any deals today? In fact, never mind closing. Are we going to open any? Ha-ha! I kid, I kid. (Not really. This is dead serious.) So. How's quota looking this month? Will we be able to pay the mortgage by the fifteenth? What about car insurance? Or should we just chuck that and take our chances? What's the worst that could happen? Oh, remember that spectacular wreck we saw on the freeway last week? How much do you think that would have set us back if we were involved and didn't have insurance? OK, how much room is left on the credit card? By the way, how big is the credit card bill now? That's not getting any smaller either, you know. And how's the kid's college fund looking? Nah, it's fine; by the time that comes around, we'll be homeless anyway. Maybe we can live in a shelter like Will Smith did in that movie. Which reminds me, have we canceled cable yet? Hey, didn't the boss say she wanted to have a word later this week? What's that about?

Chris's constant companion prattles on this way every morning, through the daily ritual of toothbrushing, coffee-making, coffee-drinking, dressing, first-thing-in-the-morning emails, and even as the day goes on during visits to prospects. Like fifty million Americans, Chris makes a living in sales. And like almost all of them, he struggles with sales anxiety nearly every day.

This guy doesn't want to talk to you, Chris. Give it up. Don't you hear it in his voice? See it on his face? He's got better things to do. You're wasting his time and yours. What are you even doing? You should have listened to your father when he said to go into accounting. Or your mother, when she said, "Be a doctor. The world will always need doctors." No. Didn't we see a Help Wanted sign at the dry cleaners yesterday?

> **Like fifty million Americans, Chris makes a living in sales. And like almost all of them, he struggles with sales anxiety nearly every day.**

It's a shame Chris can't get rid of his constant companion, because Chris is a deeply honest, approachable, warm, incredibly likeable, tenacious, and loyal employee.

Managing that inner voice—the daily chatter of a negative interior monologue—is the toughest part of the job for Chris and for sales professionals in almost every field.

Fear is real, and it's based (at least in part) on real-world experiences. Beginning in childhood, we're told by well-meaning parents that the world is a dangerous place. "Be careful, Son! Don't take any unnecessary risks, Daughter! Watch over your shoulder! The world is a scary and unpredictable place!" And then some of us grow up and deliberately choose a way to make a living that's…scary and unpredictable.

Sales has many appealing aspects, but safety isn't one of them. It's always going to have cycles of giddy highs and a few terrifying lows. If sales were a sport, it would be the sort that involves adrenaline and endurance in equal measure—things like offshore powerboat racing, kiteboarding, windsurfing—the kinds of activities that seem to have been invented to sell energy drinks by the truckload. If sales were a landscape, it would be the treacherous, jagged mountains and dark, forbidding valleys where a small, intrepid group of movie characters must go to save the world.

Sales, in short, is the sort of profession that can be extremely hard on a person's day-to-day psychological and emotional state. And the greatest threat of them all is *fear*.

A salesperson saturated with unmanaged fear is a salesperson on the brink. Unmanaged fear can begin a downward spiral that can be hard to pull out of and a cycle that can be nearly impossible to break. That is what's currently happening to Chris.

One fateful day in the not-too-distant past, Chris experienced a completely unforeseen and utterly undeserved professional calamity. In a surprise move, the owners of the recruiting agency where Chris had worked for nearly half a decade sold the business without warning. And despite what the new owners had initially said about keeping local operations up and running, they didn't. With a shiny, new regional client list in hand, they, almost overnight, shut down the Southern California facility where Chris had worked.

The new owners weren't *entirely* heartless. They told their California employees they were all welcome to come join the recruiting operations at headquarters in a suburb of Chicago. And while some employees took them up on that offer, Chris, who had been living paycheck to paycheck and supporting a child as a single parent, wasn't going to go there. Even though being temporarily out of a job was devastating, the prospect of uprooting, an unreimbursed cross-country move, and the added prospective bonuses (!) of thunderstorms, snow, ice, tornadoes, wind, potholes, and snow tires weren't the kinds of incentives Chris was looking for in a job.

They were especially unappealing because Chris knew the moving van would have to be large enough to carry a third person: Chris's constant companion, the voice of sales anxiety.

To make ends meet, Chris blanketed the area with résumés and took the first job that came along. Even as the word "Yes" escaped Chris's lips, his constant companion giggled.

Here we go again! At least this time we'll see more daylight, I guess. Time to invest in some sunscreen. Is that tax-deductible?

That was the day Chris pulled out the phone, dug deep into old contacts, and called Tim.

Tim and Chris had worked together at the now-shuttered recruiting firm for a short time, overlapping for three months when Chris was starting out in the business. Chris had developed a fast and deep admiration for Tim, perceiving him to be unflappable and completely confident in his work. Lo and behold, Tim had departed to run his own recruiting firm, but the two had kept in touch through social media, and now Chris figured if Tim had cracked the code of managing the maelstrom of sales uncertainty and doubt, he might be able to offer some sound career advice that could help keep things upright and watertight at Chris's new sales gig.

"First of all, Chris, I can hear the fear in your voice," Tim said once the two had caught up over the phone. "And I'd like to help you learn to manage that fear—either turn it against itself, neutralize it, or even make it work *for* you. But first, let me tell you why you need to manage your anxiety. And it may not be the reason you think.

"Fear never sleeps. It colors everything you do, even when you aren't actively working on selling. When you go to bed at night and lay your head on the pillow, you may think sales anxiety and fear are also sleeping. But they aren't. Fear is a cunning and constant enemy. It invades your subconscious; it attacks your entire outlook on work and on life. It limits the size of your world. It draws artificial lines around what you think is possible, so it constrains the actions you're willing to consider and blinds you to a host of options that might be available to you. It even has physiological and psychological effects on your body—every moment you're awake, and even while you're dreaming.

"Fear and anxiety release the stress hormone cortisol that can cause inflammation throughout your entire body. It can make you gain weight even if you're barely eating. It can even contribute to serious, life-limiting diseases. And finally, to make matters even worse, fear doesn't work alone. It has an accomplice that will beat you down every time: expectations. The more afraid you are, the less you expect—of yourself and of the universe. You start to live in a smaller and smaller universe. You begin to settle for crumbs, not the loaf. I don't want that to happen for you, and I hear so much fear in your voice, I'm concerned it might happen without a major intervention.

"I have a few calls to make this afternoon, but this subject is incredibly near and dear to my heart. I'd like to talk with you more, although there isn't time to cover everything I'd like to discuss with you right now in one phone call. I tell you what. I have an offer I'd like to extend. Would you be willing to meet with me? I think we can get you to a much better place. In fact, I think by the time we're done, fear might be a little bit afraid of *you*."

Naturally, Chris was ready to take Tim up on that offer right on the spot.

"Hang on. There's a condition."

"What's that?" Chris asked, seized by fresh doubts.

Oh no. He's going to want money. Of course he's going to want money, because he's a professional. Nobody gives away advice for free, you simpleton. What were we thinking, calling this man out of the blue, asking for advice for free? *We don't have extra money. Where are we going to find money to pay for advice? The kid needs uniforms for school. But if he can get us over the anxiety and the fear it's going to be worth it! Well, by all means, then, the dry cleaner is still hiring. Take on a part-time job at night. Donut shops are always hiring too, right? Maybe we could sell a few things we don't need around the house...*

"You have to take me to lunch at Canter's Deli on Fairfax on Saturday."

Chris's constant companion stopped chattering.

"Oh..."

On the other end of the line, Tim could already hear the weight lifting in Chris's voice.

"Oh, absolutely. What time shall I meet you there? Tim, you're a lifesaver."

"Don't get ahead of yourself, Chris. I want you to withhold judgment until we've had a chance to sit down and talk," Tim said, then smiled to himself as he hung up the phone.

Tom Talk

Who among us can say they have never been afraid? First day at a new school? Pushing outside your comfort zone to skydive or bungee jump? Heading home to see your family for the holidays? (I saved the scariest one for last.) Chris's pent-up state is something we can all relate to, and if we had him in the room with us now, our first instinct would be to calm and reassure him. Not only have we all had moments of insecurity in our professional lives, we've also all heard the audio playing in our heads: crippling, negative chatter that burrows in like an earworm. Sort of like the music on the It's a Small World ride at Disneyland, except sung by an ex or your invalidating high school gym teacher. Chris was nervous about his impending lunch date, but he would do well to keep in mind the words of British novelist Margaret Drabble: "When nothing is sure, anything is possible." Talk to you in about ten pages. —Tom

CHAPTER 2

HOW I OVERCAME SEVERE ANXIETY TO ACHIEVE SALES SUCCESS AND HAPPINESS

The following Saturday dawned sunny and clear, drenched in the pure Hollywood tones of yellow, orange, green, and blue. Chris enjoyed the drive to Canter's, even as his constant companion chattered away from every direction.

This is ridiculous. You know there's nothing wrong with a little dose of realism. If you don't get your hopes up, nothing and nobody can disappoint you. You're wasting your time with this. You could be spending the next few hours with your kid. By the way, do you know what your kid is getting up to while you're out chasing psychological snake oil? Think about that over your lox plate.

The palm trees swayed gently in the breeze as they do pretty much every Saturday in Southern California as Chris and Tim pulled up to the deli at nearly the same time—Chris in a well-loved and well-maintained Ford Taurus, Tim in a new BMW. They parked on either side of a gleaming Tesla Model X, met up on the sidewalk, and shook hands, both admiring the sleek lines of the high-end luxury vehicle.

"That car is a marvel of modern engineering," Chris said. "Did you hear one of those just beat a Lamborghini in a drag race? I'd never get out of that thing if I owned one. I'd probably sleep in it."

Tim grinned. "Chris, I see you behind the wheel of a Tesla in a year. Now, you might be driving it, or you might be valet parking it; only time will tell. Let's go inside, order lunch, and start to figure out which it's going to be."

Tim liked to tease. That was one of the qualities that had immediately endeared him to Chris when they had worked together years before. No subject was off-limits, and he was also quick to make fun of himself, which meant, for the time being, Chris's constant companion kept quiet.

As they looked over a menu full of pricey, sky-high sandwiches, California-cliché wraps full of sprouts, East Coast deli standbys, smoked fish platters, and newfangled panini, Chris told Tim about the current job: walking neighborhoods, trying to sell home-improvement projects like new entryways.

"Oh, you're a door-to-door *door* salesperson!" said Tim, with a twinkle in his eye. And despite his constant companion, Chris had his first hearty belly laugh in weeks. As the waiter took their orders, the two started to talk in earnest.

"Tim, how do you do it? Even when we were working at the recruiting firm, selling seemed completely effortless for you. You seemed to be born to do it. You're utterly fearless."

Now it was Tim's turn to laugh. "Oh, Chris. I am many things. I am irreverent, irrepressible, and sometimes irrational. I am dyslexic, hyperactive, and I have the worst case of attention deficit disorder you've ever—hey, look a squirrel! But no. I am not fearless.

"I have, on the other hand, learned how not to live in a state of constant fear. I've learned to put fear in a box when I need to, taking it out to get what I want and need when I want it and need it. I've simply learned to *manage* my fear and anxiety. I overcame severe sales anxiety and built an indispensable tool kit that led to a two-decade career of success in sales. Do you want to hear how?"

Chris *did* want to hear.

"OK." Tim took a sip of his coffee. Black. Then he settled back, looked Chris in the eye, and began his tale.

"I don't tell everybody I meet this story, but once upon a time, half a lifetime ago, I wasn't in sales. Well, not traditional sales. I was a stand-up comedian in Hollywood, so I guess you could say I sold myself, one joke and one set at a time. I also made incredibly good money as an agent for other stand-up comedians—people you probably have never heard of, though. Small-time guys. The names might ring a bell if I said them, but you probably couldn't place them. Jerry Seinfeld? Jay Leno? No matter. I'll send you some internet links about them later. They might jog your memory. They did some interesting stuff back in the '80s. Anyway, as an agent, it was my job to get these guys television gigs and HBO specials."

Chris's cup of coffee had stopped halfway between the table and his mouth. The noise in the rest of the deli was deafening, but at this table, you could have heard a pin drop.

"Life was great," Tim said. "And with the money I made as a stand-up comedian, I bought and smoked pot. A *lot* of pot."

When Tim paused for a sip of coffee, Chris finally did the same and realized now would be a good time to take a breath, which had apparently been completely forgotten in the buildup to this moment in Tim's story.

"The crisis came—and there's always a crisis, isn't there?—when my pot smoking got out of control. I wasn't as on top of things as I might have been. I missed some meetings. I screwed a few things up. Finally, a show producer complained to my agency president. That was it. I was fired. *That,* Chris, was my wake-up call. They say you must hit rock-bottom to get sober, but I'm not a big fan of rocks. They're hard. And I like my nice, soft bed. I had a life. I had a wife. I didn't like the idea of sleeping on a bed of rocks. So that was enough for me. I got into recovery then and there, and I've been sober ever since."

Chris picked up the coffee cup once more and offered a toast. "To sobriety."

"Hear, hear."

As their food arrived (in portions best suited for three people per plate), Tim continued. "Once I'd gotten my personal life back together, I realized I needed to get into a line of work far removed from show

> **I've simply learned to manage my fear and anxiety. I overcame severe sales anxiety and built an indispensable tool kit that led to a two-decade career of success in sales.**

business, or I'd be risking my sobriety. That's probably enough said about that. And I was terrified, because I was burning through my savings, such as it was. Remember, I had already spent most of what I'd made during my hazy, crazy, high-flying show business days as soon as I made it. So, I knew what little savings I had wouldn't last.

"And that's when I bumped into an old friend of mine, Kenny. I asked him what *he* was up to. 'I sell engineers,' Kenny told me.

"Kenny went on to say he found companies engineers could join; the company paid him a bounty for every new hire. Then he changed my life. He said, 'You ought to come join us. You could become a millionaire doing the same thing.'"

Tim paused so they could both take a few bites of lunch and to give Chris a few minutes to chew on what he'd revealed so far. It was a very, very pregnant pause.

"Wow," Chris finally mustered. "I had no idea you'd had this whole other career before you got into recruiting."

"In some ways, it prepared me for what was to come, and in other ways, it was a night-and-day transition," Tim answered. "I'll tell you the unvarnished truth, though. Initially, selling engineers was not quite as easy for me as Kenny had told me it would be. I was hired into his firm on a provisional basis. My first assignment was to place Bob, who was a statistical process control engineer."

"What's that?" Chris asked, over a mouthful of gravy and fries. Chris was a secret fan of the combination as long as nobody was judging, and even though this was Southern California, the two former colleagues had a longstanding no-judgment rule when it came to dining out together.

"I had no idea," Tim confessed. "I was handed his résumé and told to find him a job. I was *terrified*. I was sweating. But I made the calls. Dozens and dozens of calls. Maybe even hundreds of calls. And I guess you've figured out the spoiler: I found Bob a job.

"Now, I didn't know anything about statistical process control engineering, and during the course of placing Bob, I asked him a slew of detailed questions about the field, including its origins. Who had invented the discipline? Bob told me, 'Dr. Edwards Deming.' Now, one of my first instincts and guiding principles is always go to the top, so after I placed Bob, I called Dr. Deming and told him I had just placed this great engineer who had told me all about him and statistical process control engineering. And do you know what? Deming said, 'Oh, let me introduce you to my protégés.'"

Chris's eyes grew nearly as big as the platter that held his gravy and fries. Tim continued.

"And that's how I became a nationwide expert in placing statistical process engineers. My first principle: Go to the top. Was I afraid to call Deming? Maybe. A little. OK, yeah, if I'm being honest, more than a little. Is it intimidating to cold call the guy who literally invented an entire profession? Sure. Is it intimidating to face a placement assignment without a clue? Even more so. But I chose the high ground. The view is always better from up there. And a better view is a safer view. You always see what's coming at you, even if it takes more time and effort to get up there. That's just *one* way to manage fear and sales anxiety."

Tim took a few minutes to wolf down a few bites of his own food as Chris mulled over the story so far.

"I never would have thought of doing what you just told me," Chris confessed.

No. Of course you wouldn't have. That's why he's driving a BMW, and you're driving a Ford.

"Can I ask you a crazy question?" Chris asked suddenly. "Do you ever have a little voice of doubt in your head that tells you negative things? Like, things you should be afraid of?"

That's when Tim finally erupted in his own genuine belly laugh that caused a few nearby heads to turn.

"Every single day, Chris. Every single day. It's not unusual. In fact, if people who work in sales ever tell you they aren't afraid or that they don't have some sort of sales anxiety, they're either lying, lack self-awareness, or they're addicts themselves—adrenaline addicts. It won't end well for them. But there are ways to quiet that voice down. There are ways to make that voice go to another room. There are silencers for that voice. There are methods and practices I have learned over the past twenty years that can be used to manage that voice of fear and sales anxiety. I call all those things put together the *Fear Less, Sell More* method. And after I got enough practice with those techniques and went into business for myself, I started closing many more sales and was taking home an average of over a million dollars a year using those methods. Today, my business has a client list that includes McKinsey, Deloitte, and Accenture. So even when that little voice pipes up, it's a lot easier to tell it exactly where to go."

"You have no idea how relieved I am to hear all of this," Chris said, mopping up the last of a small pool of gravy with a few fries, eyes on Tim, rapt with attention.

Tim smiled. "It's hard work; I'm not going to lie to you. These aren't mysterious techniques. Even as a successful business owner, I'm still in sales. I will *always* be in sales. I teach the people who work for me that everyone in sales is really in business for themselves. So under those circumstances, you can never be completely fearless. But you can fear *less*. And now that my business is doing well and there are people working for me, I have time to do things that are meaningful to me, like volunteer in the substance-abuse recovery community."

The waiter appeared, offering more coffee. "I'll never sleep if I have more," Chris said, "especially with so much to think about. This has been the most interesting networking lunch I've ever had."

"You'll have a lot more to think about; this wasn't just a networking lunch," Tim said, taking the waiter up on his refill offer. "I'd like to get you out of the door-to-door door sales world and over here, into mine. I see a little of myself, way back then, in you, Chris. Right now, you are operating from such a place of fear and anxiety that you are disconnected from who you are. I want to take some time and give you a few lessons to help you overcome it. I'd like to show you new ways of thinking about different facets of how you function—emotionally, psychologically, physically, and vocally—so that you can get reconnected with you.

"I know you can recruit because I've seen you do it. But I want you to become a recruiter who *fears less and sells more*. I want to see you driving that Tesla next year, not parking it. Here's my card. The address of the office is right there. Show up Monday morning at eight thirty."

Once again, Chris was ready to accept the deal on the spot.

"Wait, wait, wait. Not so fast. There's another condition."

Chris groaned inwardly.

Well, sure, of course. That makes sense. Didn't he say he had probationary employment at his gig with…what was Kenny's company called? What kind of engineers was he placing? Should I have been taking notes? Oh God, I should have been taking notes! What was I thinking? Here is this generous guy, I haven't even seen him in a couple of years, and he's offering me his wisdom and experience, and I'm just sitting here eating gravy-coated french fries…

"Would you meet me for lunch for the next eight Saturdays? We can come here again next week to start. I love the menu and it's a great spot. I'll teach you the *Fear Less, Sell More* method, and at the same time, you have to tell me how you're applying it. I want to hear how it's working as you take steps to implement the method."

Chris paused five seconds for dignity. "Tim, I think I can do that. But one question."

"Yes?"

"Why eight Saturdays?"

"I stole the idea from *Tuesdays with Morrie*."

As the pair exited Canter's, there was a new spring in Chris's step, and his constant companion was, for once, uncharacteristically silent.

Tom Talk

If this happened to you, would you take Tim's offer? It is my contention that nothing bad ever happens in a deli unless you aggregate a certain number of pastrami sandwiches and calculate the arterial blockage. Chris has definitely gotten a nice serving of career chicken soup. The thing we often forget in sales is that under many circumstances, the customers/clients need us as much as we need them. Chris is so anxious that he doesn't realize Tim is always looking for a new salesperson and that mentoring talent is as professionally rewarding for the teacher as it is for the student. —Tom

---

HOW TO GO FROM FEARFUL TO FEAR LESS

CHAPTER 3

YOU ARE THE BOSS OF YOU: MEET YOUR INNER CORPORATION

The following Saturday arrived after a whirlwind of orientation, introductions, and Chris getting down to business. Inspired by Tim's full faith, Chris hit the phones hard and was already feeling more grounded and less anxious. But Chris hadn't actually seen Tim around the office all week, was eager to catch up, and as the minutes ticked by past their meeting time, his constant companion started to chatter again.

Did we get the time wrong? Are we sure this is the right day? Where has he been, anyway?

For the first time in an exceptionally long time, Chris told the companion to stuff it. And at that moment, a text arrived.

Accident on Santa Monica. Traffic. Be there in 5. Get us a table.

Tim slid into the booth, all smiles, shook Chris's hand, and immediately launched into an ebullient greeting. "Good morning, Chris! I hope everybody is making you feel welcome. Thanks for waiting. Great booth—I love these seats that are close to the counter. The people-watching is best here, don't you think? So. How was the week? Good?"

Chris had to laugh. Tim was always Tim, no matter what. His energy, his animation, his embrace of constantly moving parts. "It was great, Tim. Everybody has been incredibly welcoming. I'm working on placing three candidates, and I think I've averaged more than fifty calls a day this week to companies that employ them. I may have an interested company or two for a couple of the candidates already. Hey, not that it's my business, but where have you been? I wanted to drop by and give you this as a thank-you for this opportunity." At that point, Chris pulled a giant coffee mug from its hiding spot under the table. The words *FEAR LESS* were emblazoned across the entire circumference.

Tim laughed his enormous, room-filling laugh. "This is one of the best things anybody has ever given me, Chris," he said, turning the mug in his hands, then placing it at the edge of the table. "Let's break it in today. And speaking of today, this is an exciting day for you. Because today, we are going to take the time to get you acquainted with you. We're going to pull yourself out of the Pavlovian maze of our hard-charging, information-driven world, just for the duration of this meal. And you're going to learn that *you* are your greatest asset. Not your computer, not your company database, not your list of contacts, but *you*. All of the parts of yourself, including the parts you may not be well acquainted with or bump into on a regular basis."

The same waiter who had taken care of them the previous week appeared, saw the oversized coffee mug at the edge of the table, eyeballed the half-pot of coffee he was carrying, and said, "I'll be right back with a full one, OK? I know you can handle it." Tim and Chris both laughed. Chris let out a sigh and relaxed.

Tim continued. "Now, a few years back, as a presidential candidate, Mitt Romney took quite a bit of static for saying 'corporations are people, my friend.' But he actually got it backward. In fact, when it comes to managing fear, it's incredibly useful to think of people *as corporations*."

Chris's face betrayed utter mystification. The waiter was back, the massive coffee mug was full of fresh java, and the pair ordered. This week, Chris skipped the gravy fries in favor of a hot pastrami sandwich—it felt like it was going to be a day for a big meal that would take a long, long time to plow through.

Tim launched into the day's lesson. "Back in the days when I first got into recovery, I noticed one of the biggest obstacles for a lot of people was the concept of a higher power. It's a huge stumbling block for some, which is a shame, because it's quibbling over labels. 'But what if I don't believe in God? But what if I don't believe in *The Secret?* But what if I don't believe in the power of that lampshade in the corner of the room? How can I turn things over to a lampshade?'

"I can't tell you how many people waste months or years of their lives because they struggle with metaphors, Chris. So I'm not going to ask you what you believe in today, because I'm going to tell you that you've actually got a higher *self,* and that higher self is a whole darned *corporation*. We all understand corporations. We see them on television. We watch films about them. Most of us have seen our parents work in them and heard them talk about them since we were tiny.

We intuitively understand how corporations work. We understand their departments and their functions. So when it comes to managing fear, I'm telling you—you can believe in your *inner corporation.*

"Today I'm going to introduce you to your inner corporation. As you become more deeply oriented toward your inner corporation and comfortable with its officers and the roles they play in your life and your work, you will very naturally start to think in terms of interacting with them as you go about your daily work life. You'll start to conceive of actions you take in the pursuit of sales as strategic decisions in pursuit of developing and growing your inner corporation. And as you do that, you will find those actions attract others who want to be in the orbit of your buzzing, energetic, rapidly expanding startup. You will also become incredibly adept at recognizing, drawing out, and leveraging relationships with members of *other people's* inner corporations.

"So, here's the deal. You already have an inner CEO, whether you have ever been formally introduced to him or not—and I'm betting you haven't. That's what we're doing today. Your CEO oversees clarifying your personal mission, vision, and values and driving you forward. More on that in a minute. You also have an inner VP of sales—and I'm not talking about selling products or services, which of course, salespeople have to do and have to know and understand. I'm talking about selling and understanding *yourself,* which requires a deep knowledge of who you are, what you want, what you care about, and so forth.

"You have an inner VP of finance and accounting, who keeps track of accounts payable and receivable and sends up flags when those things get out of balance. You have a chief marketing officer who's in charge of persuasion and storytelling. You may even have

VPs of legal affairs if you've been involved in lawsuits. You definitely have a VP of operations, who keeps all the balls in the air at any given time, from having your car serviced to getting the kid to and from school and soccer practice and making sure you get to the doctor on a regular schedule.

"Now, some of these positions may be more active than others at any given time, and some may have far more power in your inner corporation than they should if you're going to grow your corporation. Let me give you an example. How powerful is your VP of risk management right now?"

> You already have an inner CEO, whether you have ever been formally introduced to him or not—and I'm betting you haven't. That's what we're doing today.

Chris glanced down at the half-drunk cup of coffee on the table and paused for several seconds before quietly saying, "I think that VP has been running the whole corporation for at least three months. And wow. I get it. I completely *get it*. I see what you're saying. It's crystal clear. I've never thought about myself this way, but you're absolutely right. The chaos in my head is already starting to fall into orderly slots. I can see the organizational chart in my mind, and that risk manager is calling all the shots."

"That's not unusual, and I don't want you to take even another five seconds to dwell on the imbalance in your inner corporate boardroom right now, because, you know what?"

"What?"

Tim took a deep sip of his own coffee, then he smiled. "You also have a VP of human resources."

Chris had to laugh, there was no other option. "I'm beginning to like this metaphor."

"Now I'd like to get back to that other thing you brought up last week—that voice you mentioned. The one constantly chattering in the background, telling you all is doom and gloom, and disaster is right around the corner. What role do you think it plays in your inner corporation?"

"I don't care who it is or what position it holds. I want to fire it!" Chris blurted out, a bit more emphatically than was necessary.

Tim smiled. "Ah. There, I can't help you. This metaphor only extends so far, and because these are all *inner* corporation positions, let's just say they're all employees for life. But how would you handle an employee in a corporation who wandered through the office at all hours like a doomsayer, poisoning the atmosphere, telling all of the others who were trying to build something successful and amazing that they were going to fail?"

"I'd put that employee on a disciplinary plan, at minimum."

"OK, then, let's do it. But you can't write up an employee without a name. What's your nattering nabob of negativity named, Chris?"

"Huh?"

"Naming a thing gives it form and power. If you name your inner voice—the one that's trying to keep you afraid and overwhelmed— you can start to tame it. And one of the secrets to taking away a lot of its power is to give it a name that's ridiculous. The *least powerful name* you can think of. It's not a Brock or a Brooke or a Tyler or a Taylor. Those names sound tough. Starting right now, since you're putting that voice on probation, give it a name that's going to make that voice deflate every time you address it. And you're going to address it from now on, every time you hear it. *Like a boss.*"

Lunch was arriving, which gave Chris a few moments to think. Memory banks were accessed. Recollections of absurd movies were scanned. Tim could almost see options being considered and discarded. And then, Chris's eyes lit up and he smiled.

"Fluffy."

"Fluffy?" asked Tim.

"Fluffy was my pet turtle when I was five. Fluffy was about an inch and a half long. And if I remember correctly, I think I set Fluffy free in the backyard one day and never found him again. Or her. I was never quite clear about whether Fluffy was a boy turtle or a girl turtle."

Tim replied, "Maybe Fluffy was gender-neutral." Several people sitting at the lunch counter turned around to see two men in a booth roaring with laughter.

When Tim had wiped an involuntary tear from the corner of his eye, he said, "You are an exceptionally good student, Chris. 'Fluffy.' That's a great name if you want to take away *all* of the voice's power. I don't think Fluffy will be around long. In fact, this Fluffy may join your original Fluffy in the land of the lost after a while.

"Now let's talk about something else that's incredibly important in this metaphor. It is your *parent corporation*. And this time, I'll show you mine first. My own father was an incredibly successful CEO. He was a man with immense intellectual gifts and drive that, to this day, I still cannot begin to wrap my head around. But he had extraordinarily little empathy; what he possessed in IQ, he lacked in EQ. Because we are all products of our parent corporations, I modeled my own professional behavior after my father's without much conscious thought when I was younger, right down to his vocal mannerisms, pitch, and rate. We'll talk more about that some other day.

"Sadly for me, this also spilled over into my personal life. I didn't develop or extend a great deal of empathy to my family either. And because I was *me,* not *him,* I ultimately couldn't sustain that style of interaction. I burned out. When we fail to thoughtfully and consciously separate from the values of our parent corporations and don't base our actions on alignment with our pure selves, it creates unsustainable dissonance and distress. I don't think you know this, but there was a time I had to walk away from everything for a while, do what aboriginal Australians call a 'walkabout,' go find myself, do a lot of therapy, get to know my own inner corporation in all of its depth and breadth, and find out who Tim really was.

"What I discovered was that Tim isn't a wholly owned subsidiary of his parent corporation. Tim's inner corporation has a much more connected, caring, and giving way of moving through the world than his parent corporation. Tim had to do a very hard thing—he had to separate and spin off from his parent corporation and create a whole new inner corporate culture in order to create a sustainable, healthier way of interacting with clients, employees, friends, and himself. And once he did that, he started attracting the kind of sales success he'd always wanted.

"So, it's funny and a bit ironic. We spend our entire childhoods shaking our fists at our parent corporation, longing for independence and saying 'you're not the boss of me!' Then we grow up, we go out into the world, and suddenly, we *are* the bosses of ourselves. Today, I am the boss of me. Just as *you* are the boss of *you.* Let's be completely honest—that's a legitimately scary proposition, isn't it? We'd all be insane not to have a bit of fear. 'Adulting' is tightrope walking without a net. It's mountain climbing without ropes. There's nobody to turn to when things go wrong. When we fall and skin our knees now, there's nobody to run to who can make things better. No wonder so many people go through their days in a state of hyper-vigilance, looking over their shoulder, waiting for something bad to happen. Right?"

Chris had been nodding along the entire time. "I really love everything you've been saying, and it makes so much sense, Tim. If I think of myself in terms of an inner corporation, I can already see a way to start untangling the thoughts that sometimes clutter up my head. Even this morning, before you got here, I was thinking, 'Oh no. Tim's not here and he's always so punctual. I wonder if he still wants to do this. Maybe he doesn't. I wonder why. Maybe he thinks he made a mistake. Maybe he won't show up at all...' Oh, wait! No! That wasn't me! That was Fluffy. Fluffy had better watch out, or Fluffy won't have much of a future with this company," Chris laughed.

"See? See how powerful it is when we give our inner fearful voice an absurd name?" Tim smiled, digging deeper into lunch.

"Do I have to limit my inner corporation's organization chart to traditional corporate roles?" Chris asked.

"You tell me. It's your corporation."

"Well, then, *heck no!* I want a chief empathy officer. I want a manager of enthusiasm. I want a VP of accountability. I may end up with twenty-five positions. And I tell you what—I'm also hiring an auditor for the next few months who can keep checking in on me to make sure my parent corporation isn't exerting undue influence on my executive team. They wanted me to be an accountant or a doctor. Oh my gosh! Can you imagine? I *hate* blood—and I hate spread-sheets even more."

Tim nodded approvingly. "Sounds to me like your inner auditor was already hard at work even before you met me, then. You just hadn't been introduced yet. See, that's the spirit. These are all internal relationships with parts of yourself. We don't create these relationships with our inner corporations—they're *already there.*

"To manage fear, all we need to do is recognize them, name them, and use their power. Once they have names or job titles, we can call on them when we need to enlist a disciplinarian, a cheerleader, a stickler for detail, or what have you. We can tap them on the shoulder and use them to manage ourselves. We can lean on them and leverage them any time we need them, because we know they're there. If some of them are weak, we can put them on personal improvement plans. To mix metaphors egregiously, it's almost like having a whole green room full of actors at our beck and call at all hours of every day.

"Our inner corporations are personnel who work for us. We activate them when we need them. In the beginning, it's a very mechanized, conscious process, but with practice, it becomes an unconscious skill. And we all can choose how deeply we want to get into the development of our inner corporations, like with any skill. It's like cooking, or dancing, or studying karate. Some people are happy to dabble, to be hobbyists. Some are happy to achieve a green belt, while others get so much out of the discipline, they want to go all the way to black belt. It's really up to you.

"In the *Fear Less, Sell More* method, everything is like that. I am going to introduce you to a lot of concepts; you can go wide or deep. You may decide one, two, or five aren't for you at all. My goal is to put them in front of you for evaluation and testing. You must decide what works for you. Your only job is *not to reject anything outright.* Eventually, you may even decide you want to hire a brand-new research and development department and explore whole new ways of restructuring and reorganizing yourself. I certainly have. That's the secret to the system, actually. Never stop learning new things, never stop finding new paths, never stop creating new cracks in the sidewalk for new roots to sprout."

Chris motioned the waiter over for refills on their beverages, to give Tim a break from talking and to take a few moments to digest—both lunch and the enormous metaphor of the inner corporation. "Thanks for the coffee. Can I get a box to go? This pastrami is almost as oversized as that mug," Chris said to the waiter.

"Be right back," the waiter replied.

"I'm going to have a board meeting on the way home, and you can rest assured, Fluffy is not invited," Chris told Tim as they boxed up their leftovers.

"Fantastic," Tim said. "Next week, let me know if you've hired any additional personnel, and I can't wait to hear about Fluffy's first performance review."

Tom Talk

Some of you may find thinking of your personality like a corporation as disquieting and impersonal. After all, we are flesh and blood with dreams and emotions that fluctuate, whereas the only things that go up and down in a corporation are its profits and elevators. The inner corporation does have an important advantage, though: it doesn't pay taxes. But then again, neither does General Motors. I find most salespeople are very emotional. Even if they aren't by nature, the stress of the job will make them so. Inner corporation is a way of managing your own personality with empathy and objectivity. Just remember, when every morning begins, you are a startup. Who knows? By the end of the day you could be Fortune 50. —Tom

CHAPTER 4

SIGMUND FRAUD: ALL THE STUFF WE TELL OURSELVES THAT'S NOT TRUE

The following Saturday rolled around, as Saturdays do, and it had been a rough week for Chris. Every phone call had led down blind alleys to brick walls, rejection, and "I wish I could help, but I can't."

Momentarily succumbing to the whispers of the worst judgment in the world, Chris picked up the phone and seriously considered trying to call off his meeting with Tim.

Luckily, "Hey Tim, I have a crushing heada—" was as far as Chris had gotten in the text message window before an incoming text from Tim interrupted.

> Chris—last minute change in plans. Meet me at
> UCLA Ronald Reagan Hospital, 11 a.m. Lobby.

A hospital? He's in a hospital and you were going to try to cancel? Just because you're feeling down? Holy get-over-yourself, Chris.

"Fluffy, I'd appreciate it if you took the day off," Chris said aloud in a strong, measured, decisive tone, then finished his coffee and set about fully waking up, showering, and getting on the road for the Saturday meetup.

In the lobby of the hospital, Chris and Tim exchanged handshakes.

"Is everything OK?" Chris asked, appraising Tim from head to toe and relieved to find nothing outwardly broken, bandaged, stitched, or attached to a visible IV pole.

"Oh, I'm fine, thanks for asking," Tim answered. "I was getting tired of the deli, and I have other business here, and then I realized this would be a good place for us to start our weekly appointment for a few other reasons. Thanks for being flexible. But tell me the truth—were you maybe just a little anxious when you got that text?"

"Come on, Tim. You don't get a text saying, 'Meet me at the hospital' and think 'Oh, of course, because that's where they serve the best frozen yogurt in the city,'" Chris admitted.

"That's a fabulous answer. Do you know why? Because it's *honest*. Walk with me," Tim said.

They set off together, Tim striding with purpose, carrying a bouquet, Chris following along, completely in the dark but trusting there was a good reason to be there. Tim continued, "I've found that honesty, especially honesty *with and about* yourself, is the first, last, and only requirement for constructively managing anxiety and fear. So congratulations. We both knew the honest answer to that question. The fact that you were able to say it out loud, without any sort of self-consciousness, means you're already one step ahead. You're well on your way to getting all the way through this process and mastering the *Fear Less, Sell More* method.

"I'm feeling more philosophical than usual today," Tim said. "We'll get to the reason why in a minute. A huge part of it, I must admit, is where we are. Can you feel it? We're standing in the middle of one of the places where the entire circle of life literally happens every minute of every day. In one unit, babies are born. In other units, people are on the way to their final exit. And in rooms all over this hospital, patients and their families are going through every extreme in between.

"There is a lot of fear here. A lot of anxiety. Most of it is the kind that is the rawest, the most real, the most inescapable, the most undeniable there is. It's tied to our mortality. There's no more genuine source of anxiety and fear in the whole of human experience. That's what Sigmund Freud taught us, among other things. When I start to feel fear or anxiety related to something less serious than the things people are dealing with here, I try to keep this place in mind to get some perspective."

Chris nodded and kept walking. They were approaching the maternity unit.

"And here we are," Tim positioned the bouquet high in front of his face with a flourish. "My sister just had a baby. I'm going to drop in, give her this, and see the new arrival for just a few seconds. Meanwhile, though, while I'm in the room, I also wanted to give you *this*." And from his jacket pocket, he produced a pacifier.

Chris crooked his head and stared at Tim, baffled.

"Look, I know you had a tough week," Tim said. "I know we can be our own worst critics. I know you're probably beating yourself up. I know you may have even felt like crying from time to time. Every baby in here has the same feelings. Think about it; a baby has just gone through a terrible separation. Everything that baby has known for the past nine months just changed, traumatically. She's lost everything she's ever known. She was nestled in a safe, dark, beautiful, warm place, floating and protected. She had it made. All she knew was quiet and peace, and she had her own rent-controlled studio apartment, no neighbors, and free cable. And then she was born! Now she's surrounded by light and noise and chaos, and she can't understand a thing that's going on around her. Nobody can explain it either, because she can't understand language. My gosh, no wonder babies cry. How terrifying. Do you blame them? I don't. Their fear is real. Their sense of loss is real. So, hey, I figure if babies can take some momentary comfort from closing their eyes and sucking on a pacifier, I won't be the one to judge them. And I won't judge you either."

> There's no more genuine source of anxiety and fear in the whole of human experience. That's what Sigmund Freud taught us, among other things.

And with that, Tim handed Chris the pacifier and disappeared around a corner into the maternity ward, leaving a perplexed but thoughtful Chris turning the pacifier over and over, examining it only superficially before shrugging and placing it in a pocket, allowing this unexpected lesson about life, change, and the trauma of birth to soak in.

Fifteen minutes later, Tim was back, all smiles. "Let's walk a bit more while we're here."

"Is everything good with the new arrival?" Chris asked.

"Everybody is healthy and happy. Thanks for asking."

The pair made their way out of the main hospital, and Tim picked up the discussion as if there hadn't been an interruption at all.

"Sigmund Freud—now *there* was a guy who had a lot to say about the human mind, anxiety, *and,* speaking of pacifiers, things we suck on," he began, which caused Chris to snort out loud. "I sometimes refer to him as Sigmund *Fraud,* mostly to be funny, which probably isn't fair, because psychology as a field wasn't even thirty years old when he came up with most of his theories. But you must hand it to him. His ideas about the id, the ego, and the superego were pretty groundbreaking."

Chris pulled the pacifier out of his pocket and gestured with it. "Indulge me. It's been a long, long time since I took any kind of general education classes, and I don't think I took Psych 101. I've heard the name my entire life, but I probably couldn't actually define those terms if you held a weapon to my head."

Tim was happy to oblige (with the explanation, not the weapon).

"Freud said we all have an unconscious part of our mind, which he called the *id,* that lives for one purpose and one purpose only, and that is to seek immediate gratification—either to achieve pleasure or to avoid pain. Other than that, the id is…well, kind of an idiot. It has no grasp of consequences or logic or outcomes. It just *wants.* That's all. Babies, when they're born, are pure id. They want food, they want sleep, they want to be picked up, they want comfort—they *want.* And what they want, they want *now.* We indulge them because there's no way to reason with them.

"Later, as babies begin to grow up, they start to realize, 'Hey, there are things and people in the world who are *not me,* and then there is *me.'* That is the beginning of the development of the *ego*—

the self-aware part of Freud's theoretical personality triad. The ego is still trying to avoid pain and seek pleasure—it's still totally in the 'me' business. It's just trying to do those things in ways that are a bit more practical and defensive. The ego gets consequences and logic. The ego recognizes if you try to gain pleasure in ways that create logical blowback—say, through taking somebody else's ice cream, for instance—you may end up getting a thwack on the head. You can reason with the ego. And so, the ego is capable of saying to the id, 'Don't do that thing you want to do right now. It'll be counterproductive. Don't steal Suzie's ice cream *while Suzie is looking,* because you will get caught, and you will get thumped on the head.' The ego is completely invested in self-preservation. It has no larger sense of right or wrong."

Tim and Chris exited the main hospital and walked outside.

"Ah, here we are. Destination number two." Tim sat down on a bench outside another building on the hospital campus. A sign read, "Resnick Neuropsychiatric Hospital at UCLA."

"Let's just hang out here for a few more minutes and I'll finish with Freud. Then we'll go where I really wanted to take you today."

Chris took a seat and they soaked in the sun. "Sounds good to me."

"Any questions about the ego or the id?" Tim asked.

"No, I think I've got those down. Id is pure *want.* Ego is *want* but with a layer of *don't take unless nobody's looking.* By the way, remind me not to send my kid to Sigmund Freud Preschool," Chris answered. Tim chortled appreciatively.

"Preschool is exactly where we're heading next, to meet the *superego,*" Tim said. "The superego, according to our friend Freud, is basically what the rest of us call a conscience, but it's not something we sprout naturally. If you left a child alone and never exposed him to adults, he wouldn't ever develop a superego, because the superego is the set of rules about right and wrong that are learned from parents and authority figures like teachers, society, and cultural rules and norms. The superego is formed by healthy children as they go through life looking up to role models. They stop deciding to steal Suzie's ice cream, not because Suzie might thump them on the head, but because it would be *wrong*. Because it would hurt Suzie. Once they've achieved that level of awareness, *boom!* Superego! They've become aware that *people outside of themselves have feelings too*.

"But then, according to Freud, when the superego develops, the ego gets stuck in the spot of peacemaker, smack dab in the middle of the id and the superego. And that, according to Freud, is where anxiety is born."

"You sound dubious," Chris said.

"If I sound dubious, that's because this is *all a metaphor*, and it's useful as far as it goes, but let's never mistake the map for the territory. I'm oversimplifying here, but yes. Freud suggested anxiety was the result of the ego failing to make peace between the id and the superego. So, he said when you become an adult, your id still wants to metaphorically steal Suzie's ice cream. And your superego says you can't. And your ego can't figure out a way to make the two sides stop arguing. The result is anxiety, which makes you neurotic. Then you go into psychoanalysis for a few years, or maybe the rest of your life, to fix your neurosis."

"OK, yes. I'm dubious too."

"Thankfully, our understanding of neuropsychological science has come a long way since our friend Freud." Tim gestured at the hospital in front of them.

Chris stared.

"OK, well, now for the news flash. For the most part, the field has moved on. Far, far away from Freud and his theories. Did you know he also thought that babies derive sexual pleasure from their mouths from the time they're born through eighteen months and their anuses from the age of eighteen months through the age of three, and that people can somehow get 'stuck' in those stages, and that's what the terms 'oral retentive' and 'anal retentive' mean?"

"Wait, what? Why did you tell me all of this stuff about Freud, then?"

"Because sometimes you need to really look hard at where you've been and where you are right now to understand you don't want to stay there anymore. Also, because the concepts of the id, the ego, and the superego are still useful, even if a lot of his other concepts have long since been discarded by other schools of psychology. To this day, you'll still hear people talking about the id and the ego and the superego when they talk about motivation and inhibition."

Chris stared at the hospital. "You're killing me."

"I'm not. But now that you mention it, that is, in fact, the biggest, ugliest, most primal fear any of us have, isn't it? When you get right down to it?" Tim was uncharacteristically serious for a moment. "We're done with this hospital campus. We can go now. But I wanted to give you some context about the rest of what we're going to talk about today. See, the biggest thing we all fear is mortality. Freud recognized it and he articulated it, and bless him for acknowledging it. We can thank him for being insightful enough to shatter the taboo and to formally come out and say, 'Yes, humans, we all fear death. Let's stop pussyfooting around and just get it out there; let's make it a part of the study of human psychology.' He did us that favor. We could throw away everything else he ever said, and we'd still owe him a round of applause for that.

"Now, at the same time, he did us another favor. In contrast to everything else we fear—everything else we have anxieties about—they're cakewalks, right? There are real things to fear. Hurricanes. Dog bites. Getting dressed in the dark and putting on two shoes that don't match. We can, and we *do*, get through all of those, one way or the other. Somehow, we always manage to put one foot in front of the other. We get through the *territory* we fear, no matter how scary our minds have made the *map*.

"Let's walk. I want to show you something else today. Want to ride together? No need to take two cars."

They strolled across the hospital campus to the parking garage, and Chris was thoughtful. "What do you mean when you're talking about maps and territory?" Chris asked.

"You know on old maps how mapmakers seemed to be unable to resist filling them up, even when they didn't really know what was out there?" Tim was pulling out of the campus and heading toward the freeway, into the unknown.

"Those spots where cartographers sometimes used to draw and write 'Here Be Dragons' when they literally *didn't know* what was out in the middle of a body of water, or a giant desert, or a stretch of unknown land? Same thing. We fear the unknown. And the funny thing is, it's *going to be there*—or not—whether we fear it—or not," Tim said, heading onto the I-405. "Those things are the actual territory we need to travel through. So, there's either an ocean, or a mountain, or a desert, or a dragon. We don't really know, but that's what's out there, one way or the other. If, for some reason, we need to travel through or to the territory, we'll find out what's there once we get there. We can choose to make that journey awake or asleep, joyfully or terrified. Some of us may even be able to approach unknown lands with no emotion at all, ready for anything that comes our way, like it's a great adventure. But our minds create the *map* of the territory.

"Tell me, have you ever gone to a place like Disneyland with somebody who's terrified of thrill rides?"

"Oh, *ugh,* yes, my ex's mother. It was awful. We spent the day in line for rides she couldn't bring herself to go on because she had convinced herself *something* would go wrong, and the rides were all going to kill us. Every single one. Splash Mountain was going to malfunction and crush or drown us. Big Thunder Mountain Railroad was going to fly off the rails and we'd fall to our deaths. I'm not sure what she thought the Indiana Jones ride was going to do. She probably thought the giant boulder would break loose and roll over us." Chris was obviously reliving a traumatic day at the Magic Kingdom in vivid detail. "My ex and I eventually felt so terrible after we'd gone on a few rides while leaving her behind that we left after about half a day, because my mother-in-law's crippling anxiety meant it was either that or we'd spend the whole day on kiddie rides, spinning in teacups. Even Dumbo was probably a stretch. It goes up in the air."

They were on the I-10 when Tim replied. "OK. Your mother-in-law was drawing a terrifying mental map of Disneyland. She was telling herself a lot of things that simply weren't true. Disneyland is real, but your mother-in-law's map of it wasn't. And she's not alone. People tell themselves all kinds of stories—about real territory, mind you—that simply *aren't true.* 'The plane I'm on will crash and fall out of the sky because we just hit turbulence,' or 'My spouse will leave me for somebody richer/more attractive/more interesting than I am,' or 'I will never see another dime of income again.'"

Chris shifted uncomfortably in the passenger's seat.

"Oh. Did I hit a nerve?" Tim asked.

"Honestly?"

"*Honestly.*"

"You know you did," Chris answered.

"Thank you for saying so. I'm here to help."

Tim drove on and Chris wondered where they could possibly be going.

"So what scary things have you been drawing on your map about sales calls this week?" Tim asked.

Chris sighed. "OK. Fine. I've told myself nobody wants to talk to me."

"That's good. I mean, that's not *good*, but you're identifying some of the things you need to erase from your map, because that's your creation, Cartographer. It's not *real*. You know one of the things we say in the rooms where I go to stay sober? Fear is just 'False Evidence Appearing Real.' OK. What *else* is on your map?" Tim was rapidly approaching downtown LA.

"I sometimes hate dialing the phone," Chris admitted.

"Why is that?" Tim asked, taking an exit.

"Because I don't know what I'm going to hear once somebody picks up, and I'm not in control of the outcome."

"Aren't you?"

"I don't control what happens once they pick up the phone," Chris replied as Tim started to hunt for a parking spot.

"No, you don't. That is absolutely true. But you're in control of making the call after that. And the one after that. And the one after that. And the one after that. You're in *complete control.* I mean, the person on the call you're on at any given moment is somebody you can hang up on. At any second. Right?"

"Well, when you put it that way…"

"I'm drawing graffiti on your map. And I just came up with a great idea for next week."

Tim, who seemed to have manifested the best parking karma in the universe, was now parking the car outside Los Angeles's biggest architectural movie star—the Bradbury Building. "Let's go inside. I want you to take a good look at some territory and think about maps a bit more."

Chris got out of the car and stared at the exterior of the building, which looked as humdrum and unremarkable as most brick buildings built in the same era. "Why are we here?"

"Follow me inside." Tim walked through the front door.

"Oh my gosh, I've seen this place before," Chris breathed, staring upward at the glass atrium and ironwork balconies.

"I know you have. But where?" Tim asked.

"Movies. Wasn't it in *Blade Runner*? Yes! That's it! It was so… it seemed so much bigger, and so much darker! And wasn't there water dripping from everywhere? Wait, wasn't this place ancient and decrepit and broken down and scary and falling apart?" Chris was examining the well-maintained interior in something just short of astonishment.

"See what a good set dresser can do?" Tim replied. "There's nothing scary about this place. It's elegant, isn't it? In fact, it's so elegant it's been used in plenty of movies that aren't scary or dark at all. In fact, remember that romantic comedy with Zooey Deschanel and Joseph

Gordon-Levitt, *500 Days of Summer*? There were scenes filmed here. Did you recognize it when you saw it in that film?"

"I have to confess, I didn't," Chris admitted, blinking up at the enormous skylight.

"And that's another difference between maps and territories. One of those films used light, shadows, props, and camera angles to make this territory seem like a place you *really* didn't want to be. Another used the very same things, in the very same building, to make it seem like a lovely, even *romantic*, setting. You and your ex had a fantastic time when you strapped yourself into the thrill rides at Disneyland. Your ex's mother couldn't even begin to approach those rides to experience them. She was too afraid to get near them. Now unless we're talking about those super primal things—the things going on at Ronald Reagan UCLA hospital that Sigmund Freud said it's natural for humans to be afraid of—fear and anxiety are maps, not the territory. They're overlays. They're stories we tell ourselves. They're related to real things, sure. But they are stories and pictures and props and camera angles we invent to dress the set. And a lot of the time, the maps we draw are far more frightening than reality."

Chris was walking through the lobby, absorbing the elaborate filigree ironwork overhead. "This place is truly beautiful."

"It really is, isn't it?" Tim said. "Wouldn't it be a shame if people went through their days thinking of it as a dark, wet, crumbling place just because they saw it that way in a movie once?"

"I get your point," Chris replied. "So the territory is different from our maps of the territory. We must go through the territory of life one way or the other. There's no point deciding there are dragons around every corner. And when it comes to the human mind, we're still figuring out *that* map too. Sigmund didn't have that market cornered."

"*Now* you've got it!" Tim started to applaud, but the echo was insanely loud in the echo-prone space. "Oops." He smiled, a bit sheepishly, as the guard handing out historical brochures about the building startled. "Do you still have time for lunch, or should we call it a day?"

"My head is swimming and my kid has soccer later, so we should probably head back so I can get my car from the hospital, but thanks, Tim. Today has been quite the roller coaster," Chris said. "My mother-in-law would have *hated* it."

They both laughed and headed out into the sun.

"We'll be back in this neighborhood another Saturday, just to let you know," Tim said. "I hope you like baseball."

Tom Talk

Hospitals can be scary, don't you think? The kind of place we don't want to be within one thousand miles of until we are in dire need and then it's, "How *long* till we get to the *hospital*?!"

Perspective is so often situational. The hospital can be a withering reminder of our mortality or a haven of miracles where lives are saved and bodies repaired. It all depends on our circumstances. The same polar extreme can exist with our clients. Sometimes we feel they are destroying our sanity and killing our business, yet with one positive phone call they can be transformed into career saviors and virtual ATMs. Do we apply those Freudian divisions of our brain to the concept of staying neutral and leaving room for positive changes in our client interactions? We must, because when fear and judgment creep in, the id, ego, and superego might as well be the Three Stooges. Solution? House those three parts in the inner corporation under chief insight officer, employing the spirit of Sigmund Freud as a 1099. —Tom

FEAR IS YOUR FRENEMY: FALSE NEGATIVES, FALSE POSITIVES, AND THE LOCUS OF CONTROL

The very next weekend, Tim and Chris stood outside Dodger Stadium. "Let's talk a bit more about the illusion of control," Tim said.

Chris had had a great week. In fact, it had been a fantastic week. Two of the people Chris contacted at Tim's firm had landed jobs, which had Chris walking on clouds. "You were right, Tim. I had to power through my fear. I just had to make a few adjustments to get here."

"Not so fast, there, Chris. We are just getting started, to tell you the truth, and that's why we're here. Let's go."

It was a game day, and the home crowd's mood was palpable. Hot dogs, burgers, popcorn, and beverages of every sort roamed the stands in the capable arms of their barking vendors. As Tim and Chris found seats far enough away from the action that they could take it all in while still talking without disturbing serious fans, they dug into some less-than-nutritious (but delicious) ballpark food and a couple of colas.

"Behold, America's pastime—the most superstitious sport on the planet," Tim said.

"You can say that again," Chris replied.

"OK. Behold, America's pastime—the most superstitious sport on the planet."

Chris grinned. "You know, at first I didn't know what to expect from these weekly meetings, but I have to admit, I'm enjoying them. You make them fun. I didn't expect job training to make me laugh as often as it does."

"Well, for one thing, you can stop thinking of this as job training," Tim said, stretching his arms a bit and flipping his sunglasses down so he could watch the players warm up on the field. "It's so much more than that. It's a way of moving through the world. It's a way of approaching life itself. Tell me—*other* than work, what sort of things do you tend to worry about? What do you get anxious about? What do you fear?"

Chris took a bite out of a chili dog and gave this some thought. "Well, I worry about my kid, obviously. Everybody who has kids worries about them, right? I worry about the world in general and whether my kid will have a worse life than mine. I worry about my parents, now that they're getting older. You know. The usual."

"And what can you do about those things?" Tim asked, as the players began to take the field for the first inning.

"I've considered wrapping my kid in bubble wrap until the age of twenty-one, but I don't think that'll work," Chris half joked. "But no, seriously? I'm doing my best. You can't be everywhere at all times, so I lean on technology. Trust but verify, right? A family plan for all our phones, even my folks. All our media is synced to the cloud, so I see what everybody is taking photos of, for example. I can always see where everybody is with an app. That gives me a lot of peace of mind."

"Why?" Tim asked, nonjudgmentally.

"Because, I guess, you can't be too careful?"

"What about when your mom steps out the front door and isn't carrying her phone one day? What if there's a bus coming? I mean, it could jump the curb. The brakes could fail. Or somebody on the bus could be carrying a weapon that discharges unexpectedly. There are a whole lot of dangerous situations in the world that you simply can't control, Chris.

"You're doing a lot to try to anticipate and control real dangers that you perceive to be reasonable. I'm asking you to consider whether perhaps you're allowing yourself to be lulled into a false sense of security, or a false negative, because everything you've been doing, has been based on a specific set of fears you are capable of imagining. And you're imagining them as a means of trying to *gain control over a situation you ultimately don't control*, which is the universe rolling on its merry way without you.

"I'm asking you to think about the extent to which some of the things you worry about every day are actually within your control. I'm not offering answers; I'm not the guy for that. I'm just asking the question. Oh. Also, while I'm asking that question, I want you to notice that none of the baseball players are stepping on the foul line. That's the baseball equivalent of breaking a mirror."

"Yeah, I know that," said Chris, who hadn't made much progress on the chili dog.

"Do you think a foot on a foul line actually affects the outcome of the game?" Tim asked.

"Oh for heaven's sake, no. That's ridiculous. It's just one of the funny little superstitions of baseball."

"Of course it is. But baseball isn't all that different from sales in a lot of ways, is it? Baseball players have their rituals and routines, and they won't change them for fear of breaking a streak. They'll wear the same socks for weeks. They won't shower or shave or bathe. They'll eat only fried chicken on game day, or they'll use the same bat, or they'll go through a choreographed series of tugs and taps and pulls in the batter's box before they really get down to the business of getting ready to hit. Even the seventh-inning stretch is a superstitious ritual.

"This game doesn't have a score yet, so I think it's safe to talk about this, but you don't mention a no-hitter or a perfect game when it's in progress, right? All those rituals are there for a reason—they're *false positives*. They're ways of establishing false notions of control over a situation that will ultimately either come down to skill or luck. These guys are better at this game than 99.99 percent of the rest of the human race, and they still want more control over the outcome of the game. That's pretty amazing, when you think about it."

Chris had to admit it was.

"Great salespeople can use fear, which, I hope you're beginning to understand, is with us from the cradle to our final breath, in the same way. I don't think the majority of baseball players *genuinely* believe that if they wear the same athletic cup they wore during high school games, or take showers so hot they could scald themselves on game day, or any of the hundreds of other rituals that play out before or during games will actually *cause* them to play better. But the illusion of control—creating that illusion builds confidence, and confidence can affect performance. So *that's* real. How's that for a paradox?"

"So wait. You're saying superstition and the illusion of control aren't real, except when they are?" Chris took another bite of the chili dog and sat back, well and utterly confused.

"I'm saying for the sake of performance, when the outcome is truly out of their hands, if a ritual is something these players can do to calm their nerves and help them focus all of the skill and training and practice that makes them one of the best players in the world on the game, then fear is their friend. But if they get to the park and they find that somebody stole their lucky hat? Or the bat they've hit the last three home runs with breaks and that completely shatters their mental focus? Then the superstition is no longer beneficial. Fear is their enemy. It's always about the *effect* of fear on performance. For baseball players as well as for salespeople."

"So what you're saying is, fear is not my enemy."

"It could be. Could also be your friend. It depends. I guess I'm saying, depending on how you use it, fear is your *frenemy*. And speaking of frenemies, how *is* Fluffy these days, anyway?"

Chris, who was taking a sip of cola, narrowly avoided an ill-timed snort. "Fluffy has been better behaved since I decided she's a she, for one thing. For another, Fluffy now has an imaginary crib she sleeps in, because after our trip to the maternity ward last week, I decided Fluffy is an infant with an exceptionally large vocabulary. When she gets really noisy, I tell her to go to bed. And I tie a bonnet on her head."

"Now is that any way to treat a friend?" Tim chuckled.

"Fluffy isn't my friend. I think Fluffy is the side of my fear who's definitely my enemy. Is there a side of my fear who can be my friend?" Chris asked, as the crowd roared for a base hit. Tim and Chris joined in.

The announcer chimed in, "Dodgers are one for five this season on Saturdays at home."

Chris said, "Hey, even the announcers do it!"

Tim agreed. "Baseball statistics are full of meaningless and non-predictive numbers like that, and it gets even crazier during the post-season. If you settle in during the World Series, you'll hear some stats that will make your head spin and make you wonder *who decided to even keep track of things like this?* 'The home team is three for four in games that start at six thirty in the Central Time Zone.' Really crazy stuff. But again—it's the illusion of control. And fans eat it up as well, at least in part, because it gives *them* an illusion of control by proxy. Would you rather watch a game with no announcer, with no clue about what the outcome might be, or a game in which some-body is telling you, 'OK, this guy coming to the plate now, he's a strong hitter, and odds are better that he's going to hit the ball than the guy who just struck out'?"

"Definitely the latter."

"Absolutely. We humans hate uncertainty. It goes against our nature. Back to maps and territories—a lot of people would rather see 'Here Be Dragons' than a big blank spot. Making peace with uncertainty—making friends with fear—that's its own kind of training and skill-building. Also, by the way, was dialing the phone easier for you this week after your two big deals closed?"

Chris broke into another big grin as the baserunner stole second and the crowd exploded. "I was chasing the adrenaline this week after that, to tell you the truth, Tim. Nothing could get me down. Everything was just falling into place, and every conversation felt like it could go someplace good."

The batter caught a bit of the ball for a foul, and the home crowd gasped.

Tim asked, "Do you think any of those conversations were false positives?"

"I'm not sure what you mean," Chris said. "Not in the way we've been talking about them. I didn't get up and turn around three times before dialing the phone, if that's what you're talking about. I didn't feel like I needed to use a lucky pen or stick to my script word for word or else the call would fall apart."

"In sales, a false positive is a slightly different thing than in baseball. It's clinging to *good* signals for too long before moving on to the next thing. It's looking for signs that there may be a sale here, trying to qualify a lead too long, maybe, or spending too much time with an unqualified lead. Fear of taking a prospect to no. Throwing good time after bad. Have you ever thought a call went spectacularly and then you never hear back? False positive. It's chasing a yes long after you should have accepted the no, because yes is like a drug, isn't it?"

A home run punctuated Tim's declaration more perfectly than anything had a right to, and the crowd's celebration went on for what felt like minutes. When the noise settled back down to reasonable levels, Chris answered.

"I see what you mean. There may have been a call or two I stayed on for fifteen minutes longer than I should have last week. I figured I'd see if I could get more contacts or leads from them because they were pleasant, and after the last few weeks, just having somebody who was willing to talk to me was nice. Those calls are always a welcome break, aren't they?"

"Well, you just said it yourself. A false positive is a *break*. It feels good, yes. But if you aren't actively moving a prospect toward yes or no, even subtly, you're standing still—and that's a disrespectful use of the prospect's time as well as your own. In sales, just like in baseball, you must either be fielding or hitting. Time spent on false positives in sales is like the time these guys spend tugging on their caps and drawing symbols in the dirt in the batter's box to establish their own illusory sense of control and security. When time is your number-one asset—and it *is*—you may want to reconsider that investment.

"And what about *false negatives?* What about those? Have you been dealing with any of those? This week or last week or any week since you've started?"

"What would those look like?"

"Oh, those are the easy ones. 'I've called twenty-deep into this list with no luck, so the list is garbage.' Or, you get somebody on the phone and instantly you think, 'This person wants nothing to do with me other than to get off the phone right now.' That's usually a false negative. You have no way of actually getting inside somebody else's head and knowing what they think, after all. You can only observe and hear what they say. Your phone call isn't generally that important in somebody's day, one way or the other, until you say something to make it important to them, in a good way. That's within your power. That's within your control. See?"

"I do see. But then, if control is something that's an illusion, why am I staring at a field full of baseball players who all follow elaborate superstitious rituals that create the illusion of control? And listening to an announcer who also feeds into that, surrounded by fans who buy into it? What's the deal here?"

"I thought you'd never ask," Tim said. Meanwhile, a double play ended the top of the first.

"In psychology, there's a concept called the *locus of control*. That's Latin for 'location of control,' because heaven forbid we use English or professors wouldn't have jobs, right? The idea is this: Everybody assigns credit or blame *somewhere* for events in their lives. Some people tend to have more of a bias toward an *external* locus of control, and some people tend to have an *internal* locus of control.

"If you view the world through an internal locus of control, you believe you make things happen. You choose to get up in the morning, get dressed, get in the car, take a certain route to work. If you get into an accident, you may even perceive that as within your control—'Dang it! I should have taken Sepulveda this morning. Then I wouldn't have been here at this very moment, and I could have avoided this fender bender!' That would be an example of an extreme *internal* locus of control.

"An *external* locus of control is totally opposite. That's actually a very technical and polite way to say somebody has a *victim mentality*. 'Everything always happens to me. Why does the universe have it in for me? I was just driving along on Sepulveda and *wham!* Out of nowhere! This car hit me!' People with an extreme external locus of control don't feel responsible for anything that happens to them, even if they caused it. They could literally step out into traffic, get run over, and they'd blame the traffic. The *world* just happens to those with an extreme external locus of control.

"Now, baseball. Baseball is a funny game. You'd think that a game of incredible skill and finesse which requires so much technical ability and practice—which these guys have all been playing since they were tiny kids—would naturally lend itself to players forming an *internal* locus of control, wouldn't you? You'd think these players would approach every game with the inherent belief that their own actions can and do have more effect on who wins the game than a bunch of superstitions, right?"

"Totally," Chris said, watching the pitcher neatly send down a batter in three.

"But it's also a game where, honestly, not a lot happens for huge stretches of time. Here's my theory: When these guys are standing around in the outfield, keyed up, knowing at any second something monumental and game-changing could happen, but it doesn't, that causes anxiety, right? They're just waiting. The worst thing that can possibly happen to you when you're incredibly skilled and highly trained is *nothing*. That causes stress. The brain wants to handle that nothing and turn it into something. No other sport has baseball's elaborate psychological rituals, because no other sport has room for them. Hockey? Soccer? Basketball? Football? Those guys are moving constantly. Those games are active. Those athletes don't need to keep their minds engaged in the game during hours of downtime, waiting for the few seconds when their expertise and skills could be the difference between winning and losing. So I think in baseball, paradoxically, all the players' superstitions and rituals are a way for the players to stay intensely connected to what's happening on the field and regain a sense of internal control. The game isn't just happening *to* them. The rituals and traditions and superstitions are all active attempts to take personal control of the game—they're signs that professional baseball players have an internal locus of control when it comes to their team, their sport, and the outcome of every game."

"That's wild," Chris said. "It's basically the inverse of what I'd have thought."

"Exactly. So what I hope you're taking away from today, other than a great chili dog, a day at the ball park, and an enjoyable game I hope the Dodgers will win, is that I'm not passing any judgment on what people

> **The worst thing that can possibly happen to you when you're incredibly skilled and highly trained is nothing. That causes stress.**

do to leverage their anxieties or fears. There's no right or wrong, ever. There's no absolute. Fear can be your friend. Fear can be your enemy. An internal locus of control can be extremely liberating because it means you're in control of your life and your destiny. But an external locus of control is appropriate when, say, somebody develops a serious illness or a giant boulder rolls down a mountain during a hike and nearly crushes you.

I'm not a huge fan of the kinds of pop psychology that say, 'You attract everything that happens to you in life,' because in some cases, those can be cruel and blame genuine victims of completely unforeseeable circumstances. It's all about context, and it's all about how we choose to *respond*. Our responses to events and to other people are the source of a great deal of our power and our abilities in life, including the ability to excel professionally—whether that's in sales, in sports, in acting, in comedy, whatever. In fact, next week, let's meet up at an acting class. I'd like you to learn more about how to consciously engage your body and your voice as a sales instrument. For now, let's settle in and see how this game turns out."

Tom Talk

By now, we have all accepted that fear is a part of any salesperson's life. With all due respect to President Franklin Roosevelt, there is more to the notion of fear than just saying, 'We have nothing to fear but fear itself.' Come on, Mr. President, fear itself is actually pretty scary! There are pandemics, recessions, judgmental in-laws, nonrefundable airline tickets, and when it comes to baseball, your star pitcher needing Tommy John surgery. Human beings have plenty to fear. But making peace with uncertainty—with fear—is more than training and skill-building, as essential as they are. It's making friends with yourself. There's no absolute right or wrong. It's all about accepting what you can and cannot do. Your strengths and limitations. Since I know one of my limitations is self-editing, I will stop right here. —Tom

CHAPTER 6

THE ACT OF SALES: WHEN THE CURTAIN RISES, UNDERSTAND THE PERFORMANCE

C hris and Tim met up the following weekend outside a tiny building tucked away on a side street in West Hollywood. The Art Deco sign announced it was an acting school: The Acting Space.

"Oh, so you want me to *act* like a salesperson?" asked Chris. "Fake it until I make it, right?"

"Today, we physically knit together what goes on inside with what goes on outside," Tim said. "When you're talking as a salesperson with anybody, including those gatekeepers you only speak with for a few seconds, you're engaged in a performance. Always. In my view at least, sales is *always* performance. We are always acting, and it's always live. Sales isn't a film. You can't yell, 'Cut!' and start over again. It's improv. So being open to learning some of the craft of acting is a worthwhile endeavor.

"With every new line, every new question, every new performance, something can and will change. That's the only thing you can predict about sales: You're living in a changing scene every second. You're reacting to your partner in the scene, even if—maybe especially because—your partner doesn't know that he or she is also living in a scene. That's why we're here. Today you're going to get a sneak peek behind the scenes.

"I took *a lot* of acting lessons when I was younger. Maybe one day you'll decide you want to pursue that too to refine your own skills. For today, I just want to open your eyes to the possibilities."

> **When you're talking as a salesperson with anybody, including those gatekeepers you only speak with for a few seconds, you're engaged in a performance.**

Chris looked slightly less terrified. Slightly. "Do I have to do anything?"

"For now, just watch. Later, though, you may surprise yourself," said Tim. "Sales is always an improv performance. Learning about the psychology of acting can serve everyone in sales. Speaking of sales, how did last week go?"

"I'm actually feeling pretty good, all things considered," Chris answered, voice lighter than it had been in weeks. "I'm making connections—well, let me rephrase. I'm making connections *once I get to somebody I can actually make a connection with*. I'm calling my way down a few enormous lists, working my way into a couple of new, huge companies, feeling my way around, running into a lot of gatekeepers. Getting a lot of low-level hang-ups and clicks, though, you know. Even though they aren't personal, they still get to you. Just a little. Even though my superego tells my id it's nothing personal, the ego still takes it personally from time to time." Then Chris chuckled, produced the pacifier from his pocket, and held it up. "When I start feeling sorry for myself, I know what to do."

"You suck on that thing in the office?" Tim asked, incredulous for a moment.

"Are you kidding me?" Now it was Chris's turn to look dumbfounded. "No. People would think I'm out of my mind. But I have kept it with me this week, because when we started this, I made a commitment. I'm all in. And it may sound crazy, but when my ego wants feeding, I pull this out for a second and look at it. In my mind, I tell my ego to suck on this. That makes me smile; I get my perspective back. And then I'm in a good place to make the next call."

"You're making great progress, Chris. You've done a lot of internal work so far. Mindset is critical to success in sales, and overcoming fear and sales anxiety begins there, but it doesn't end there. Anybody who tells you that you can merely *think* yourself to sales success by internally managing sales anxiety hasn't stopped to wonder why there are so many unemployed psychics, am I right? Internal action must be matched with external action. That's part of the reason why we're here today."

"Yes, why are we here?"

"Today I am going to introduce you to a brilliant acting teacher, who is also a full-time working stuntwoman here in Hollywood. She uses many techniques, but all of them are designed for the performers to contact deeper places within themselves and to be more present," said Tim.

They entered The Acting Space and were greeted by Carey, a reflective redheaded woman dressed in a black blouse and black slacks (which conveniently served as near-perfect camouflage in the totally black-painted studio space in which the day's acting workshop would take place).

Tim and Carey greeted each other warmly; it was obvious to Chris this was not the first time the two were meeting.

"Carey, I'd like you to meet my latest sales protégé, Chris. And thank you again for allowing us to come to today's class," Tim said.

"You're both so very welcome," Carey answered, in a voice that simultaneously soothed and intrigued. "Come on in. The workshop I'm running today is a small, invite-only group of friends. We're working on a refresher on being in a state of inspiration. As an artist, you need to receive all the inspiration you can from the people you are working with, as well as your own creative resources. And in sales, you want to be in a state of inspiration, too, so I want you to participate."

Now Chris looked genuinely terrified.

A final pair of actors entered the room, and the whole group began to gather around Carey in a circle, seemingly by instinct.

"OK, everybody, let's get to it. I want to push, pull, throw, lift, or crush; what is the significance of these?" asked Carey.

"The psychological gestures that Michael Chekhov* taught," said a student.

"That's right," replied Carey. "How the urges of push, pull, throw, lift, or crush are done adds a quality that changes the verb into

---

* The Michael Chekhov Acting Studio in New York City suggests five basic gestures: push, pull, throw, lift, crush, according to Leonard Petit in *The Michael Chekhov Handbook*, Routledge, 2010.

unlimited variations. For example, a *violent push* becomes a shove while a *tender push* is encouragement. A *slow pull* is to seduce, but a *quick pull* becomes a jerk. All possible actions can be found in these basic urges living in the human being. Many of these become manifest in the womb, and all in early infancy, without being taught."

A familiar-looking young man, tall and attractive in that archetypal Hollywood-hopeful sort of way, spoke up. "We aren't interested in elaborate theories of acting that require drawing on memories of emotions people had experienced already. Those were needlessly complex and overly taxing to actors. Besides, audiences can't see you thinking or remembering. They can only see what you *do*. So we study the urges, these basic building blocks of physical action and expression."

"That's right," Carey said. "Everything we do, one way or another, comes down to one of those urges. Not a lot of refresher work needed today, I see." Carey took a dramatic pause before continuing.

"There is a question that Michael Chekhov would ask actors: Are you primarily a radiator or a receiver? A radiator is someone who has their energy flowing from their core to the periphery, like Clint Eastwood in *Dirty Harry*. A receiver is someone who draws people to them to gain their power, like Marilyn Monroe in *Some Like It Hot* or James Dean in *Rebel Without a Cause*. Incidentally, both were Chekhov actors. Now I want you to pair up."

"Tim! Tim!" Chris half whispered, half hissed. "Who's Michael Chekhov? I feel like I'm in that nightmare where it's the end of the semester and you suddenly have a final exam but forgot to study for it!"

Tim reached wordlessly into Chris's pocket, pulled out the pacifier, waved it three times in the air, then dropped it in Chris's hand.

Chris surreptitiously returned the pacifier to his pocket, now its permanent home, as Tim fixed him with a not-unsympathetic gaze.

Tim raised his hand, which surprised Chris. He wasn't used to seeing Tim behaving with deference, which spoke volumes about the respect Tim had for Carey.

"May I?" Tim asked Carey, who waved permission with one hand. "I want to thank you all for welcoming us into your space today and allowing us to observe and work with you. My friend here is completely new to this, and I wanted him to see and experience the late Michael Chekhov's power in action. He was quite a teacher, and I'm thrilled his methods are still being taught around the world."

Carey took the reins back. "One great exercise Mr. Chekov offered is called making friends with objects and spaces. This has to do with our own emotional response to intimidating environments. So if a person walks into a space and becomes intimidated, that isn't a good situation. Many actors experience that with auditions. But Mr. Chekhov literally says to the objects, 'Hello, table. Hello, light bulb. Hello, rug that I just tripped over. I'm so humiliated, but thank you for being my friend.' And the exercise is to practice that in the classroom today."

As the students began the exercise. Carey took Tim and Chris to the farthest corner of the room. Chris stayed as close to the wall as possible, trying to become exceedingly small.

"Michael Chekhov wasn't just a teacher," Carey said. "He was a working actor—a brilliant one. He was a star. He descended from theater royalty. His uncle, Anton Chekhov, was one of Russia's most famous playwrights, and he studied acting with the legendary Konstantin Stanislavski, who invented The Method—the kind of acting we all just think of as 'acting' today but which was absolutely revolutionary when a young guy named Marlon Brando strutted into Hollywood and took the town by storm. As has already been mentioned, Chekhov didn't believe in a lot of theoretical fluff. He thought acting training should connect actors to their emotions and their psyches through their bodies, that it should all function as one inseparable unit. When people say, 'Get out of your head,' they're telling you to do what Chekhov said: Stop thinking so much. Get into your body. Just *be*. React authentically to what others offer you. Stay present in the moment, and use your imagination to create responses."

Carey again used silence to capture her students' full attention. "Let me give you an exercise called imaginary body," she said. "Think of your imagination as completely unlimited and like a super cloud you can download images from. They all exist. They're in the cloud already, so you don't have to make them up. You don't have to feel like you need to be creative. Now imagine you can just beam down a body like the transporter in *Star Trek*. Tim, put on an imaginary body of a resistant buyer. Chris, you put on the imaginary body of whoever you think is an ideal salesperson. In this case, you're stepping into the imaginary form of a successful salesperson. So that leads us to psychological gestures. And it's an entire movement with a clear beginning, middle, and end that anchors into the person, the thinking forces, the feeling forces, and the willing forces."

And with that, Carey walked away to interact with the pairs in the rest of the class.

Chris was staring at Tim through saucer eyes. "I. Have. No. Idea. What. I'm. Doing." The whisper came through gritted teeth.

"All the better," Tim said with a gleam in his eyes. "What part of 'Get out of your head' didn't you follow?"

The next few minutes were, hands-down, the scariest minutes of Chris's life, flying without a net or a safety harness, doing things never before done in a room full of experienced actors working their psychological gestures as the experienced, fearless pros they were.

Chris froze. But then Tim reached down into the space between them, bent his knees, and, with his fingers, grasped an invisible giant platter upon which Chris just happened to be standing. Tim looked up at the ceiling. Then he made intense, unsmiling (one might even say defiant) eye contact.

Finally, still looking Chris straight in the eye, and with great apparent effort, he *whooshed* the invisible platter (apparently still containing a now-invisible Chris, because Tim broke eye contact, and his gaze followed the whole thing) upward into the black ceiling, into the sky, possibly even into the stratosphere beyond.

Then he stepped forward and reestablished a decidedly normal, everyday, undefiant form of eye contact that simply said, "Your turn."

In that moment, Chris *got it*. He took a deep breath.

Chris's version of ideal salesperson involved miming a huge, confident, hearty handshake in the space between the pair, had they been allowed to touch. It was punctuated with an enormous bear hug at the end.

Over the course of the rest of the workshop, Chris and Tim observed as much as they participated. Carey was fine with that. So were the rest of the actors, who continued to work with other skills in the Michael Chekhov tool kit. Through it all, Chris was shocked to discover that the anticipatory anxiety that had defined the early minutes of the day was completely, totally, and utterly gone, replaced time and time again with a range of emotions tied to the physical gestures the group was working on. Having experienced elation to confusion to relief to grief, by the end of the class, Chris was wrung out.

"Tim," he said, as the class wrapped, "this has been revelatory. Once I got over my initial freeze-or-flight reaction, I wasn't as uncomfortable with this as I thought I'd be. I mean, I don't think I'll be quitting my day job to go into acting, but I have to admit something embarrassing: I always thought actors just had better memories than other people so they could remember their lines. And I thought they had an innate ability to laugh or cry convincingly on cue. I had no idea so much work went into acting. I'm ashamed to admit that right now. I thought acting was all about being handsome or pretty, not screwing up your lines, maybe knowing the right people. It's so much more than that."

Tim arched an eyebrow. They were interrupted as the familiar-looking Hollywood-handsome young man, who had spoken up earlier approached.

"I'm sorry to interrupt, but I heard you laugh a bit ago, and even more than your faces, I recognized that sound," the young man said to Tim. "And I just wanted to say, thank you so much for that incredible tip a few weeks ago. It actually helped with rent last month—more than you'll ever know."

Canter's Deli. Their waiter.

Tim smiled. "I had a feeling you had a dream bigger than filling enormous coffee mugs," he said, extending his hand and shaking. "Back when I was taking acting classes regularly, the first thing I learned was that I really hated waiting tables. Which means you're already ahead of the game—well, you're ahead of me, at least, because you're really good at that too. It was the least I could do. Nice to meet you again. What's your name? And to paraphrase one of my favorite movie lines, are you a *good* actor or a *bad* actor?"

"Tim!" Chris said. "We just watched this man smash a whole planet with his pinkie. Silently. Trust me. He's a *good* actor."

After class, Chris and Tim went to debrief at a local coffee shop. After the waitress took their order and departed, Chris flashed a huge Cheshire cat grin to Tim.

"Did you see what I did there with the server?" gushed Chris. "I'm noticing everything in this weird way, like I have X-ray vision or super hearing. I never listened to the tone in someone's voice, I never responded so intuitively to what the person said. A word can be a question, a demand, a form of affection."

The coffee arrived and Tim took a healthy swig. "I hoped the outcome of this class would be you giving up your obsession with saying every word perfectly," said Tim. "Knowing the right phrase and having seventeen closing lines memorized will not catapult you to success. Reading people and connecting to them, without using your brain to manipulate them, will get you to the promised land."

"Ah," said Chris. "So the trick is not to act like a salesperson, but to sell like an actor."

Tom Talk

Much of the preparation an actor does before performances looks nothing like what happens on stage. It's bigger, broader, louder, magnified, outsized. The same principles apply to sales. When you're working on closing skills with a partner or a coach, for example, don't be inhibited. Go big. Get extreme. Refuse to back down. Hold your ground.

The point of acting training is to make performance look natural and easy to the audience by removing the disconnect between thinking and reacting. "Getting out of your head" is actually the opposite—it's connecting the head with the rest of the body, eliminating the artificial barrier between the two, allowing physical motions to create emotion without allowing overthinking to come between the two. The same holds true with the act of sales.

Lessons in improv, acting, and other performing arts can help reduce sales anxiety by extending your skill set into creative areas that tap into parts of the whole human body that are not typically taught or explored in sales training.

Acting training is great—just don't get carried away and make the mistake I did early in my life and try to be a professional actor. That is, unless you like constant rejection, living on macaroni and cheese, and spinning a sign on a street corner for a living. —Tom

FIGHTING FEAR WITH FUN: THE UPS, DOWNS, HIGHS, AND LOWS OF SINGING IN THE SHOWER (OR YOUR CAR)

"So, tell me, Chris, exactly what are you afraid of, or when do you have anxiety?"

The pair had broken their usual standing Saturday afternoon appointment and were walking on a clear, starry Saturday night toward a hole-in-the-wall nightclub.

Tonight, Tim had promised, wouldn't be work at all. Tonight would be *fun*.

"Oh, you know, the usual," Chris answered. "Some days—most days—I get through just fine. Then on other days, if something isn't quite hitting on all cylinders, then everything strikes me as something to fear. Fluffy starts whispering, *You're not smart enough. Prospects are going to call you out for not knowing something. You're boring. You're doomed in this career. You'll never get through enough nos to get to enough yeses to make this work.* Those are the days when I feel like I'm swallowing a cotton ball along with every sip of coffee and my teeth are boulders and nothing I say will quite come out right. To be honest, there have been fewer and fewer of those days since I've started working with you, but they still happen."

Tim nodded and said, "That's a voice you hear loud and clear, isn't it? Fluffy's, I mean."

Chris shrugged. "I've been telling Fluffy to go away a lot, and Fluffy does, in fact, oblige more often than not nowadays. But yes, I'd know that voice anywhere."

"Tell me—what does Fluffy sound like?"

This brought Chris up short. "I...don't know. I've never actually thought about it. I guess Fluffy sounds like *me*."

"Interesting."

"Why 'interesting'?"

"Not important at the moment. Might be later, might not be. Anyway, we're here. Let me pay your cover tonight. It's going to be a *great* time."

It turned out Tim was being literal. A poster at the front door announced the main event: *Karaoke with the Greats.* "Karaoke? Tim, I've never been able to carry a tune in a bucket. A bulldozer's bucket. Not talking about a beach bucket here."

Tim let out one of his big, trademark, bellowing laughs as they strode into the club. "That's OK, because this isn't straight karaoke. It's karaoke with training wheels, essentially. You don't have to sing alone—you can sing right over the original vocal track if you want to. It's a marvelous confidence-builder for people who don't think they're the next incarnation of Lorde, even *with* auto-tune."

Chris looked confused for a second and then asked, "What if my idea of fun is to just sit back and *not do this?*"

Tim's head swung from side to side in perfect time with "Chances Are," which the emcee was currently singing (without the benefit of Johnny Mathis's original background track—and he was doing an uncanny impression, it must be said). "Sorry, Chris, but one of the ways to *fear less*, in general, is to take a leap into the great unknown and do things that scare you when they have no actual potential for negative consequences in the real world. Look around. Do you know anybody here?" Chris looked around. Chris admitted he knew no one.

"OK. So what possible negative consequence could singing along with a classic recording have?"

"I'd...be embarrassed if I did a bad job."

"What's a 'bad job'?"

"I told you. I have a terrible voice. I can't sing. I sound like a dying moose when I try to sing. Not that I've ever heard a dying moose, but if I ever do hear a dying moose, I promise you, it will be what I sound like when I try to sing."

"And you think after most of these people have had a few more drinks, anybody is going to actually care if you don't hit all the notes precisely right? Speaking of which, I'm going to get myself a tall seltzer. Do you want anything?"

Chris contemplated all the available forms of liquid courage but also remembered Tim's earlier revelation about getting sober decades earlier. "I'll stick with what you're having. Thanks."

The emcee was warming up the crowd with standards and captured both the vocal and physical qualities of the original artists. Chris sat back and enjoyed the singing and the easy banter and watched as other patrons, some looking distinctly less than eager, flipped through the karaoke catalog and placed their names on the evening's list.

"Did you ever notice Johnny Mathis always sounds like he's singing into a broken microphone?" Tim asked, depositing icy, sparkly waters in front of the duo as he returned from the bar. "Ch...ances... aaarre..." He briefly demonstrated what he was talking about, dropping the beginning of each syllable and Chris chuckled, getting the crux of the joke immediately.

Tim continued, "Our voices are as individual as our fingerprints. They're just as unique. The emcee did a good job of capturing that quality in Mathis's delivery. I'd know who he was singing even if he were doing a song Mathis had never sung, based on that vocal quality alone."

When the emcee wrapped up his intros, the first brave karaoke singer of the evening stepped up to the mic; she had selected Amy Winehouse's version of "No Greater Love," which, let's face it, was an audacious choice to break the seal. When she opened her mouth, a knockout sound came out. It may not have been the kind or quality of sound people would pay to listen to by the tens of thousands, but by gosh, this woman was in the spotlight right now, and she was owning it.

Tim was smiling. "This lady gets it."

Chris was not smiling. "What? She sounds *nothing* like Amy Winehouse!" Chris whispered, hoping not to be overheard.

"Sounding exactly like the artist isn't the point," Tim said. "Embodying the artist's attitude, emotion, and spirit—that's what's happening here. There's only ever going to be one Amy in the world, but right now, this woman is simultaneously inhabiting the space Amy carved out in the world and the one she lives in too, because she's listened to Amy enough to be able to step into that space and command our attention from within it. *Listening* is the foundation of *connection*. She is absolutely killing it, even if she may be flat on this note or sharp on the other or coming in too soon on another."

They sat back and kept listening to not-Amy as she fearlessly went vocal-for-vocal with Amy, and slowly Chris's lesson for the night began to reveal itself. Not-Amy was having a blast. She didn't care what anybody in the crowd thought of her singing abilities. She was up there for herself, belting out smoky chanteuse phrases for her own satisfaction. Anybody watching and listening could tell this song and this artist spoke to something deep inside her. It was obvious this evening, this moment, this song, was one of the high points of her week, and her reward was a healthy round of applause.

Tim's was as enthusiastic as anybody's. "What a treat. I'm glad she broke the ice, because you saw and heard the same thing I did: She's not a great singer, but she has spent a lot of time with that recording, you can tell. When she sings it back, even if every note isn't perfect, she encapsulates the emotion and the attitude of that song. Really great stuff. Now, who's next? Oh. Barry Manilow? Let's move outside, chat for a few minutes, and get through this. Do you ever sing along with music when you're alone?" Chris admitted that might happen from time to time.

"So if you're singing alone at top volume in your house or in your car, Chris, I'm going to let you in on a little secret: Nobody is there to judge you, except maybe your kids, and news flash—they're judging you anyway. The great thing about singing is some people take enormous risks and spend huge sums of money to fear less—they race cars and motorcycles, or base jump, or climb mountains. Well, between last week and tonight, I am telling you—you can go to Everest, or you can learn to put yourself in spots that terrify you almost as much by getting yourself out there, playing with your own voice and body. You can learn to improvise and act. You can put in earbuds, listen to a song in your house or car, learn every note, and sing along to it. Maybe you'll get a little hoarse, but you don't have anything else to fear, at least physically. You certainly aren't rappelling backwards at a ninety-degree angle from the face of the planet. Which of those options sounds less scary now?"

Chris smiled. *Perspective.* "I'll take the karaoke."

"Fabulous. I knew you'd see my way of thinking. Because you, Chris, are a great student of life and of fearing less. Shall we head back in? I think I just heard Tony get shot at the Copacabana, so this song is almost over."

"Hang on just a second, Tim. I just told you I already sing to myself sometimes. So tell me again, why do I need to sing in front of all these people?"

"Tonight you may not, although if you do, you're going to be showing me a willingness to crash through your fears without a net. But in a longer-term, larger sense, your voice is as much an instrument for *fear less* selling as your brain. You can expand your vocal range and the things you can accomplish with your vocal instrument by *listening intently* to the artists who have perfected the use of their own voices, then mirroring their delivery. In this, as in nearly everything in life, what you pay attention to, you perfect. Normally, we think of singing and speaking as two different skills, but they're actually two different points on a continuum—the human voice can say 'ah,' in one short burst, or it can sustain a note, 'aaaaaaaaaaaaaaaaaaaaaaahh-hhhhhhhhhhhhhh.' Same voice. Same skill.

"I used to sing jazz and scat as a much younger man—did I ever tell you that? That's probably a story for another day, but when you study vocal music, you learn that the trained voice imparts its own emotional notes and tones and hues and colors to every utterance. You can say or sing the words 'burn' or 'fire' or 'go' in a hundred different ways and every time, those words will convey completely different meanings.

"That's what your own tonal explorations can do when you sing along with great singers. And it can be fun. Especially when it's low-risk—singing in the car, singing in the shower, singing alone in your home, or singing in low-stakes situations like karaoke with the greats. Come on. We just heard a man butcher 'Copacabana,' for heaven's sake. How much worse could you possibly be? You'll put your own stamp on something. I know you will. Go over to the catalog. Pick something. You can do this."

Chris cracked a smile. It was true. Chris could do better than "Copacabana."

As a new song stylist attacked "Don't Stop Believin'" with verve and vigor, Chris quickly scribbled a song title onto the night's list on the way back to their table. Then Chris caught up with Tim, who was returning with a new set of seltzers.

"See? The spirit of adventure and fun replenishes you. The spirit of defeatism, anxiety, negativity, and anger drains you over time," Tim said to Chris as he sat down. "Think about the kind of songs that embody the qualities you want at your fingertips as you make sales calls. Think of ways to describe them, then find songs that match those qualities. Do you want more heat? Maybe learn a song that sizzles. More fierceness? Try something that makes you want to roll down the windows and howl at the moon. Do you want more devil-may-care self-assurance? Start with one song by Dean Martin. Listen to it five times. Ten times. Let it soak in. Let every note speak to you. You'll quickly get past its novelty and find yourself listening more closely to nuances. What *is* it that makes Sinatra sound like Sinatra? What vocal qualities make Amy Winehouse unmistakably Amy? How do vocal impressionists capture the essence of a performer within a few notes and gestures?

"Once you've listened so many times you can actually hear a song in your dreams—heck, even before that point—start by singing along in the shower. Great acoustics there. Then sing it on the freeway. Try to match its feeling, its emotion. Don't worry if you don't get all the notes right. Singing is an emotional exercise—as I said before, it's about listening and connection. When you're singing a great song in the style of a great artist, you're absorbing, reflecting, and amplifying human emotion through your own voice. You're doing an enormous amount of work on the psychological and emotional side of sales.

"Here's the secret I want you to carry away tonight, Chris: Everybody has a little bit of Frank Sinatra inside, just like everybody has a little bit of Taylor Swift inside. Everybody has a little bit of Adele, a bit of Elton, a bit of fill-in-the-blank-with-the-great-sing-er-who's-going-to-make-your-next-call-easier-to-make. Coaxing that person out of yourself is as easy, or as hard, as giving yourself room to play with that person's voice, wherever it may be trapped inside you. The first step is finding the emotional qualities that are missing from your repertoire, finding music to match, and making the time to learn to sing along to it. Let those voices out. Let the notes out. Let the words out. Let it rip."

"Well, this *is* certainly shaping up to be more fun for me than last week," Chris said, "because last week, I felt like I was the first man on Mars trying to communicate with aliens we didn't even know existed on the planet. This I can do. But…"

"Yes?" Tim was all patience and openness. Tim was here for the *fun* today. No pressure.

"How do I choose? I mean, I get it. I can choose to be as smooth as the late Bill Withers, or I can growl like Trent Reznor about to rip apart prey in a jungle. But how do I choose which voice or story to embody on a given day, or on a given call?"

"Each call is an adventure—whom do you want to be?" Tim asked. "You're the casting director for yourself, every time. These are all your choices. That's the great part! That's also the intimidating part, isn't it? Trusting your instincts as a salesperson based on what you're hearing in real time is one of the things that separates the wheat from the chaff. Think of developing your roster of voices as another way of giving yourself more options during calls. It's a way to develop confidence in the sales skills you are building beyond simple product knowledge and basic prospecting and closing techniques. That's how you can let go and *fear less*.

"You already know that sales, like life, is an art as much as it is a science. This isn't your first day working the phones. The biggest skill you learn when you practice the art of singing isn't actually singing—it's *listening*. What are you hearing on the other end of the line? Let that inform you. One call, you may decide the voice that will help you project the most power is a throat-shredding Axl Rose, because you're going to need that kind of fire and energy to slice and slay your way through every objection. On another call, when you really listen, the other person's voice may tell you this is going to be a seduction, and you'll reach for a very different quality of voice—perhaps John Legend, famous for being the first African-American man to win an Emmy, Grammy, Oscar, and Tony—the EGOT. I can't tell you whose vocal qualities will impart the energy you're reaching for on a particular day or in a particular moment of a particular call. The bigger your cast, the more resources you'll have to draw on. And by the way, I'm absolutely not telling you to do actual impressions, because that would be silly, especially on a live sales call. You get that, don't you?"

Chris nearly choked on his seltzer but nodded vigorously. "Um, yes, I think it goes without saying I won't be singing to clients..."

"Great," Tim said. "Just had to check because some people are terribly literal. Just like those psychosocial exercises from last week are rehearsal tools and not for use on stage, the same thing applies here. But I can tell you this: Playing with singing and voices—inhaling and exhaling the energy of extraordinary people who have already embodied the art of human communication in extraordinary ways—will imbue you with a greater reservoir of energy, capability, and insights into the characters you interact with every day in a sales job.

"When you sing along with somebody who has mastered the human voice's range, tones, emotions, and color, you are building access to a form of emotional shorthand they took years to perfect. You are, in essence, borrowing their expertise, creating a well of sensory and psychological responsiveness and sensitivity to other people via their vocal cues. These skills and sensitivities will serve you in sales and in life. If you make it a practice to sing along with the greats like Frank Sinatra, capturing his style and his attitude, you will not be able to avoid, at least momentarily, embodying his swagger and his confidence. And then you'll have that feeling at your disposal when you need it in the future. It's similar to the psychophysical acting methods we played with last week. It's a technique—a tool. A means of quickly accessing connection by leaning on a trail blazed by somebody else. Another way of increasing emotional intelligence and connection.

"I used to sing solos with great jazz singers—their narratives, their sounds, the language of their stories told through notes. To really *hear* a note well enough to match it in all of its emotional connotations—that can be like a full workout for your ears in the same way a two-hour aerobic-and-weight gym session is a workout for your body. If vocal mirroring and mimicry isn't something that comes instinctually and naturally to you, you really have to focus hard on listening—not just to the content and the words of a song, but to every breath, every sound, to the characterization and the feeling expressed through intonation.

"As you develop your ear through the practice of singing with the greats (or even the mediocre), you'll start to develop an ear for the markers of emotion in spoken language as well. Pacing, breath, word choice, volume. Every sales call you make is like a Rubik's Cube. You're listening and speaking at the same time, gathering information and discarding tactics, making a hundred decisions, lining up the colors between the person you're talking to and *who you are*. If you line up all the colors, you just might get a client. But listening— really listening—that's the basis of everything. It's why we're here tonight, because I am convinced if you aren't having fun with listening, sales will never be the right life for you. There must be joy in the life you choose for yourself, or it isn't the right life. If you honestly feel abject terror every time you strap yourself onto a roller coaster, that's not the right ride for you in the long run. A roller coaster needs to be fun if that's the ride you take every day, right?"

Chris was in genuine agreement on this point. "Absolutely."

The evening proceeded with great animation, much laughter, and enormous rounds of applause. True to his word, Tim took a turn at the mic and selected an Ella Fitzgerald song (with the vocal track turned off), scatting as only a trained scatter could scat, earning hoots and hollers and raucous cheers. Then it was Chris's turn.

The emcee stepped aside and handed over the mic. Emboldened by a night of other people utterly undaunted by karaoke with the greats, Chris accepted it with great flourish and belted out the tune, informing everyone that the end was near, that he was facing the final curtain, that he was stating his case and was certain. But there was more, much more than this, as Chris ended the song by bellowing, "I did it myyyyyyyy way!" and broke into a grin.

At a table toward the back of the room, Tim nodded along, satisfied.

When it was over and they were walking back to their cars, Tim asked, "Are you sure you don't know who Fluffy sounds like?" Chris shrugged.

"Time to give Fluffy a voice, then, too. Just like you gave Fluffy a name."

A moment or two went by, then Chris stopped short on the sidewalk, eyes wide and sparkling. "Oh my gosh. Oh wow. It's *perfect,*" Chris said, then burst out laughing.

"What?"

"It's not only the voice. It's everything. I can wave this at Fluffy too," Chris said, producing the pacifier from a pocket. Tim narrowed his eyes in confusion.

"From tonight on, the role of Fluffy will be voiced by an eight-year-old Shirley Temple."

Tom Talk

The difference between "scary" and "fun" can be a shift in attitude. There are legitimate things to fear in life—things that can hurt, maim, kill, and/or bankrupt you. Everything else is small potatoes. If it's unlikely to leave scars and you're feeling anxious or fearful, see if you can reframe the way you're feeling about a situation to think of it as an adventure or a novelty.

The point of singing (at home, in the shower, in your car, or even on karaoke night) isn't how good you sound, it's how well you listen. Like acting or improv, the real point of training in the entertainment arts isn't necessarily becoming good enough to perform in front of an audience. It's teaching yourself to be present in the moment, to hear and respond to other people in all of their complexities, and to express yourself authentically.

Every great singer offers different qualities you can draw on in your sales calls. If you want to be Frank Sinatra singing "My Way," you don't actually have to sound like him. You can capture his take-no-guff, no-apologies attitude by recalling the dozens (hundreds?) of times you've sung that song in private. Need to amp yourself up into the kill zone before a call you know is going to be challenging? Get yourself into a death metal mode before you dial. Fairly sure you're this close to closing and want to sweet-talk them in a country state of mind? Go for it. Just be prepared for the possibility of their own country song follow-up: "If the Phone Don't Ring, You'll Know It's Me."

Disempower the internal voice of fear by changing its voice. In the same way that removing your inner critic's power began by giving it a name that was absurd and diminished its authority and ability to make you feel small, find a voice that strips it of even more of its dominance. It's hard to be intimidated by an inner negativity monologue voiced by SpongeBob SquarePants. Or Scooby-Doo. Ruh-roh—there goes its power over you! Find something that speaks to you—and when it speaks, it makes you laugh at the absurdity of being afraid of the voice in the first place. It's the vocal equivalent of getting over your anxiety by picturing an audience in their underwear. —Tom

CHAPTER 8

THE FEARLESS MYTH: OUTSOURCING YOUR FEARS

S aturdays with Tim were nothing if not exercises in last-minute flexibility, Chris thought as he drove to a pancake house in an old, old strip mall out in the relative hinterlands of Los Angeles, singing along in the car with an oldie but a goodie: "Hit Me with Your Best Shot" by Pat Benatar. Compared to all the other homework, it turned out singing was the most fun.

Navigating a parking lot full of matinee moviegoers, Chris found a spot near the appointed destination and saw Tim walking toward it. They were meeting at a not-at-all-fancy-looking pancake house, and Chris was glad to have spotted his mentor, because otherwise, it wasn't entirely clear this was the right place. Chris leaped out of the car and trotted to catch up.

"Tim! Good morning! It's a beautiful day. Thanks for the text with the new address, but I've got to ask, is this the beginning of a scavenger hunt? Are we going on a quest? Why are we here? This place looks like more of a dive than last week's karaoke bar, and that's saying something."

Tim met Chris's eyes. He was more serious this morning than Chris had ever seen him. "I've got to be honest with you, Chris. Today, I need a meeting. I didn't want to break our Satur-date, and at the same time I'm going to be honest—I think there are life lessons, strength, and wisdom in the rooms of AA that can help everybody. I appreciate you coming all the way out here. Now, having said that, I understand if you don't want to come in. But it's an open meeting. That's why it's held in a restaurant. You don't have to say a word. All you have to do is listen. Are you up for it?"

"I...I don't understand," Chris said. Of all the possibilities he had ever entertained when their Saturdays together had begun, riding on a SpaceX rocket would have ranked slightly above going to a twelve-step meeting with the boss. "I don't drink. I don't smoke. I don't overeat. I don't take drugs. I'm confused, Tim. This is so outside the realm of sales I can't get my head around it."

"This is an unusual meeting. The core group has been getting together for more than forty years, and it has always met here. By the way, the pancakes? Excellent. The carpet? Probably as old as the meeting. Are you game?"

"I don't have to say anything? You're not going to ask me at the last minute to stand up and tell my life story or anything like that, the way you tend to?"

"No. That I promise. All you have to say is that you're visiting."

Chris considered for several seconds, but seeing the look on his mentor's face was all it took. "I'm game, then."

Together they walked through the restaurant and into a back room with a separate door that offered the group, still assembling and ordering breakfast and coffee, a bit of privacy. Tim greeted several people warmly, and they returned his greetings with gentle ribbing.

"Tim! Haven't seen you here in a while," an older gentleman, who may once have been in show business, offered.

"I've got to admit, it's been a rough few weeks," Tim replied.

"What, did you lose a hundred million dollars in the stock market?" the man joked. Tim smiled, but it wasn't the sort of smile that reached all the way to his eyes.

Chris shook hands and met several people while ordering coffee and chocolate-chip waffles. Tim settled in and then the older gentleman walked over and laid his hand on Tim's shoulder. In a voice low enough not to be overheard by the others, the old man said, "I think you should lead today's meeting, Tim."

When Tim didn't bat an eyelash, Chris was both astounded and deeply satisfied. *He walks the talk. Let it never be said he expects of me things he isn't willing to do himself.*

When the meeting began after a round of first-name introductions (and Chris did only say, "I'm Chris, and I'm visiting"), Tim opened.

"Hi. My name is Tim, and I'm an alcoholic. Sales can be a brutal way to make a living. It's like a riptide. If you try to fight it, eventually it will pull you under. It's *bigger* than you. It's overwhelming. Sales involves *so many variables* you can't control—its vagaries and polarities, its mountains and its valleys. If you try to brute-force your way through a sales career, I am here to tell you, sales will *break* a part of you. Sounds like something else, doesn't it? Sounds a bit like... addiction.

"In fact, philosophically, I have just recently started to look back over my career in sales the way I look at my life in recovery—as an opportunity for deep work in human connection and personal development. The work I've done with the steps through the years is personal development work. The same kind of work that makes you a better salesman. I'm reminded of that when everything in my life goes wrong.

"What do you do when you're caught in a riptide? When you're caught in the wake of something larger than yourself? You don't fight against it. You must find a way to swim with it—parallel to the shore—to draw strength from outside.

"Sales isn't like any other way of making a living. It's a demand for personal development. A calling—a challenge to find ways to connect to other people, sometimes within seconds, and to make that connection sustainable, to build trust so real and so quickly that people will *hand you their money* to solve their problems. That is an enormous burden. Sales isn't just about knowing two dozen closes or twenty-five prospecting techniques. At its best, it is a deeply moral and ethical profession, and personal development will make you a better salesman and a more sustainable one.

"I sometimes struggle to keep that perspective. I've been working with my employees to help them develop personally for years, but that doesn't mean I know it all. When it comes down to it, I don't know everything. My sponsor didn't know everything when I got into recovery thirty years ago. My professional mentorship work outside the office is something I think of as a part of service—part of my ongoing personal development. Every six months or so, I choose one of my direct reports who seems to be struggling, and I work with him or her to get past, through, around, over, or under the obstacles or roadblocks standing in the way of sales success. They don't always have the same issues. Sometimes they're too eager and they push prospects away. Sometimes they're too reticent and we need to work on confidence. Right now, I'm working with somebody with different issues.

"But that's not what I want to talk about today. Not really. I want to share something very personal with you today. I haven't had a time that's been as challenging to me personally and professionally as these past few weeks, since

> **Sales isn't just about knowing two dozen closes or twenty-five prospecting techniques. At its best, it is a deeply moral and ethical profession, and personal development will make you a better salesman and a more sustainable one.**

the last time I used. It's literally been one thing after another. My brother, who's sixty years old, just checked himself into rehab for cocaine abuse, so I guess you can say we keep it in the family. He did me the favor of reminding me where I *don't* want to go again.

"Two weeks ago, my company's biggest client, which represents about half of my business's revenues, told me they're thinking of taking their business to another vendor. I pulled out every counterargument I knew—every technique, every reason, every rationale. I went intellectual. I went emotional. I went personal. At the end of forty-five minutes, I felt that everything I'd said had been met with a cold, stony glance. I hadn't been able to come up with the superhuman feat—I wasn't able to turn this customer around.

"And despite the fact that I know everything I told you at the beginning about sales and about control, I didn't see those forty-five minutes as a chance to exercise my skills; I felt that failure as a body blow. I felt it as a death ray. It turned me into a puddle of insecurity, even though intellectually, between my ears, I know better. I allowed that phone call to permeate every other part of my life and color all my interactions with every other person who matters.

"It's such a helpless feeling, and I've been stuck in a dark spot ever since. I've been trying to hold it together on the outside. But here's the thing: We are losing that account. And when we do, if I don't find us another account of similar scale, it may jeopardize the continued existence of the company."

The room was quiet. Chris was as silent as all the others.

"So today I've come here because I desperately needed to remind myself that I've been powerless all along. All the years the company thrived. All the years we were making money hand over fist. All the years I bought amazing cars for my kids on milestone birthdays. I've never actually controlled anything other than my own actions.

"Even after three decades, I knew I had to come to this meeting today because I needed to get my perspective back. I realized that the next turn in the road is still going to come if I'm moving forward. There's no avoiding it. And as much as I want to, I can't see the next turn from here. None of us can. All we can do is accept that our road lies out there ahead, and we're on it, moving forward. Our road will take us on a journey, lead us to experiences we can't foresee. We don't *draw* our roadmaps, because we don't control the world—thank God. All we do is hold the steering wheel of our own vehicle.

"And it's so interesting, isn't it? When I step back, I can see all the ways the universe has surprised me in positive ways through the years on this journey of mine. If I had clung stubbornly to the script I was trying so hard to write for myself thirty years ago, before I came to these meetings, I would never have gone as far, never have had as rich an experience, never have led the life I've led. I'd never have built the business that's giving me such fits right now. Here I am, once again, having nearly forgotten the lesson, trying once again to cling to the script I'm trying to write today, doing the same thing all over again. What's the definition of insanity?"

Several people raised their hands and one volunteered, "Doing the same thing over and over again, expecting different results."

"Exactly. Sometimes life has a funny way of reconfirming what you already know—I have no power at all over external events. That customer had made up his mind. I haven't actually *lost* anything. I never had control over that decision in the first place. When I step back from the precipice, I realize my value as a human being isn't measured in dollars and cents but by *my reaction to external events.* And my ability to react to all these events is what I am teaching you today.

"My choice in this situation is how I react. It's the difference between dull resignation and what I call luminescent acquiescence. Acceptance comes in different flavors, different colors. You can accept things lying down or standing up, making the best of them. On a windy day, you can stay inside, you can lie down to try to be sure the wind won't knock you over, or you can grab an enormous, gorgeous, colorful kite, and you can welcome those winds outside, fly that kite, and laugh. That's luminous acquiescence. Right?

"But boy, do I lose that perspective and energy sometimes. These were those weeks. Today was that day. Thanks for letting me share."

The rest of the meeting (which was, of course, anonymous) followed the tone Tim had set. People from every walk of life and every sort of profession, from retail clerks to psychoanalysts, talked about control and the lack of it and how this fed into their own anxieties and fears about the future. They spoke of "letting go and letting God." They closed the meeting with the Serenity Prayer:

> *God, grant me the serenity*
> *to accept the things I cannot change,*
> *courage to change the things I can,*
> *and wisdom to know the difference.*

And then it was over. Tim said goodbye to everybody, many of whom it was obvious he'd known for decades. Chris lingered after the meeting was over.

"That was…not what I expected today, or any day, Tim. Do you do this with every person you mentor?" Chris finally managed to ask, when the room was clear and all that remained was silence and half-drunk cups of tepid coffee.

Tim was clearly feeling better because of coming to the meeting. He was radiating an air of calm and reassurance that hadn't been there even ninety minutes prior. "No. I have to say, you're the first person I've brought with me to a meeting. Maybe because I knew you'd be able to handle it."

"I'm not sure how well I'm handling it, to tell you the truth," Chris answered. "Those things you said about the business—they're true?"

"Absolutely true."

"And you brought me here to help me fear *less?*"

"Lying to you isn't a part of the plan. I'd appreciate it if you'd respect the anonymity of the meeting and not share that outside, but I'd also appreciate it if you'd mull over everything else that was discussed about understanding what we do and don't control and finding a way to let go of what we cannot control.

"At a certain point, lying in bed at night obsessing over things we can't control—that way leads to madness. Obsession. Addiction. Burnout. Emotional problems you can't picture and don't want in your life. Relationship problems. Financial spirals. Fight-or-flight. Illness. You can make yourself emotionally and physically ill if you latch on and obsess over problems you cannot control. You have got to find a way to outsource your fears."

"Well, I've got something I need to break to you, and it's probably going to pose a bit of a problem, then," Chris said.

"What's that?" Tim asked, all openness.

"I don't believe in God."

For once, Tim didn't laugh. He only nodded and smiled. "That's great. That's fine. You don't have to."

"But...all of that 'Let go and let God' stuff and 'God grant me the serenity' stuff.... That's not going to work for me."

"Fine. Find something or somebody that isn't 'God.' Do you believe in anything?"

"Nope. Not particularly. I don't even believe in *The Secret*. I don't believe in crystals. I don't believe in auras. I don't believe in UFOs or chakras or my inner child. I know. Let's face it—I'm a lousy Southern Californian."

"OK. Here's a question. Do you believe in other people?" Tim asked.

"Like...do I believe they exist?"

"Sure. Let's start there."

"Well, obviously. You're standing right there. I believe you exist."

"Great! OK. Now. Do you believe you know everything? Or do you believe other people can be smarter than you, more competent, more experienced, and wiser than you about some things? Especially when you get them together in a group? Say, this morning, for example. Did you learn anything from anybody this morning about how to think about control—or your lack of it—that you didn't know before you walked into the pancake house?"

"Well, yes, actually I did."

"Congratulations, Chris. You just found your higher power, and it's a group of people with life experiences you haven't had!"

"Oh, Tim, that seems semantically shifty. Are you telling me when I hear the word 'God' I should picture a room full of people eating pancakes?"

"For the purposes of today, and tomorrow, and the next day, until you find another one—if that is what it takes to get you to outsource your anxieties and your fears to somebody or something that is not yourself, because Chris, you are not that big and not that powerful, trust me—then yes. Starting today, your 'God' is a room full of people eating pancakes. Sometimes in the meetings we say, 'Your higher power can be a lamp,' but I've never actually understood that analogy because you can stand right up and turn the lamp off. A room full of people eating pancakes would definitely be more powerful than a lamp, and next time I'm at this meeting, I'm going to share your breakthrough analogy, actually."

Chris smiled. "So you're basically telling me I need to find something or somebody other than myself where I can throw my fears and anxieties about the things the world flings at me, like this news about our biggest client. Because I certainly can't control that. All I can do is hit the phones on Monday harder. Right?"

"Now you get it, kid. Your higher power, whatever it is, is bigger than your fears. Actually, if you find you're struggling with fears and emotions on a general level, you may or may not know this, but there are twelve-step groups out there for everything these days—not just for substance abuse. There's probably one for fear and anxiety. I'm just saying. Keep that in your back pocket. A group of people all dealing with that issue? Probably smarter, wiser, and more powerful than just one Chris. And in the meantime, maybe you and Jim Campbell at the office—I believe you guys get along very well—you two could team up. You may not know this, but AA was started when Bill Wilson teamed up with Dr. Bob and created the phrase, 'Recovery is one alcoholic talking to another.' Just substitute 'salesperson' and you might be on the way."

Chris finished the last of his coffee and realized there was no counterargument to be made.

Tom Talk

Being married to your own agenda can lead you to be professionally single for your career. Takers never really give. And so, they miss out on the joy and gratitude that comes from deep client relationships that can last a lifetime. Reciprocity is like oxygen for career development. With takers, more is never enough, leaving room for no one else. That's why I wrote a simple joke based on a well-known saying: The pessimist says the glass is half empty, the optimist says it is half full, and the taker says, "Are you done with that?"

The illusion of power over what happens out there in the world is just that—an illusion. The only power we have on our lives' journeys is how we react to events in them.

No matter how skilled we are, how many sales seminars we've attended, how many closes we know, how many tools are in our kit, there will be times when the nature of a career in sales hits us hard. That's the time when we need to reach out to our higher power, whatever that may be, however we understand it, and give up the fear and anxiety. Outsource the need to control to a force bigger than you. You can't control potholes or road closures. All you can do is steer.

Many of the precepts, tenets, and self-development concepts that are taught (and learned) in twelve-step programs, believe it or not, are applicable to the *Fear Less, Sell More* **method.** That's because they're essentially ideas, skills, and philosophies that aren't isolated to living a healthy life in the *absence* of drugs, alcohol, or anything else; they're actually a recipe for living a healthy, productive, rewarding life, period. They apply to managing anxiety and fear as much as they do to managing any problem that is negatively affecting somebody's ability to live as they genuinely want to. —Tom

SECTION III

KEEP ON KEEPING ON

CHAPTER 9

THE HAPPINESS BALANCE

C hris and Tim were driving together through the high desert between Los Angeles and Palm Springs on their last Saturday to an incredibly special grand finale: a charity tennis match between Roger Federer and Rafael Nadal at Indian Wells. As they drove along Interstate 10 through the Coachella Valley, they talked.

After so many weeks and different experiences designed to help Chris overcome the voice and embodiment of fear, Tim was feeling expansive and genuinely enthusiastic as he spoke with Chris.

"I want you to watch this match today, not only for the speed and excitement and thrill and dynamism of the game but also with an eye on the style and character of each player. Both players are geniuses. But I think Federer is a happier tennis player," Tim said.

"What do you mean?" Chris was puzzled. "I'm not an expert or a dedicated superfan by any means, but I've followed this rivalry for years, and I consider myself a bit of a student of the game. Nadal has passion and he's a fiery competitor. Also, I identify with him. A lot."

"What do you mean, you identify with him?" Tim asked. "He's from Spain!" They both laughed. "No, seriously. He's a prodigy. He's a legend. What makes you identify with Rafael Nadal?"

"Well, I think he's got OCD, and I do too. Can't you tell?"

"What do you mean?" The mountains outside of Palm Springs were rising in the distance as they approached their destination.

"Well, before his serve, Nadal goes through these little rituals. He does something with his shirt, he tugs on his pants. He does a set of predictable, repetitive things to make himself comfortable. And I relate to that. I understand the need to get things in order and make yourself at home mentally before you act. I *get* Nadal's approach to the game. It makes perfect sense to me. Once you've got all your ducks in a row, then you're ready to get going."

"Well, of all the things to have in common with him, I have to say that's one I've never heard before. You're a true original, Chris. But it's not something I'd ever have chosen to emulate."

"Me either! I'm not saying that's why I admire him as a player—I admire his passion, how he throws himself into every shot, and how exciting he is as a player. He's an incredible athlete. It's just that we do have that little thing in common."

"I can't argue with one thing you've said," Tim said, "But I still maintain Roger Federer is a *happier* player, and I'll tell you why. Want to hear?"

"I'm not sure being a happier player is important, but OK. I'm assuming that's why we're on our way to Indian Wells," Chris chuckled.

"Truly, you have been a good student," Tim smiled. "And I'm glad you asked. Roger Federer has lasted and succeeded longer in this game than just about anybody. At thirty-eight, he's still competing and winning multiple Grand Slam tournaments. At thirty, Nadal is already getting injured a lot. That's because Nadal muscles the ball. He dominates it. He overwhelms it. He crushes it. He overpowers it. And as great as he is, it takes an enormous physical toll to play his style of game—to create that topspin and play his game the way he wants to play it. It's not as fluid, elegant, or balanced as Federer's game. Let me tell you a story."

"I'm all ears," Chris said, grabbing a bottle of water and settling in.

"When I was younger, I had a friend who was also a prodigy like Nadal. I admired him enormously. He was one of the best players in the country—certainly in the East—and he went on to play tennis professionally. We're friends to this day. A few years back, he came out to visit me and we played a few sets. I was trying to impress him, and it didn't go so well. I was doing the muscling thing. Smashing the ball. Pounding it. I kept getting angrier and angrier and more and more violent with the ball, really throwing myself into every swing.

"When it was all over, he took me aside and he said, 'Tim, let me tell you two things. First, you're not good enough to get angry. Your whole mindset is to overpower the ball and kill it. What you're trying to accomplish when you're playing against me is, honestly, completely beyond the abilities and skills you've honed. To be angry when you're playing just shows you're out of touch with reality. It doesn't accomplish anything other than to make you play worse. If you can manage to accept your skill level for what it is, then maybe you'll be able to relax, actually enjoy the game, and be happy.'"

Chris took a sip of water but didn't say anything. He stared at the white spires of windmills rising and turning in the distance and knew they'd be arriving at their destination soon.

"So a part of what my friend taught me in that moment was about my own temperament. But the other part was technical. 'The other thing is, you're only swinging at the ball with your arm. Your back foot is stationary. You're not moving through the ball kinetically with all of your energy. Instead of only using your arm, you need to be flying at the ball with your entire body, creating a collision, moving all the weight and parts of your body in a fluid, elegant motion to create massive momentum that meets the ball to move and direct it in a moment of pure, unleashed energy. It's a different style of play. And nobody in the history of the game has done that better than Roger Federer.'"

"Huh," Chris said.

"I know. It was a revelation to me, too, but it makes sense. Then he told me Federer's style of play is more sustainable than other players' because there's less wear and tear and less stress on the body. He's as passionate as anybody else who plays the game, and he works just as hard as anybody else, but he brings an ease, an elegance, and a grace to the game. Happiness, if you will."

The miles rolled by fast at the unofficial California freeway speed limit of eighty miles per hour, and they were now pulling off, approaching Indian Wells.

"This is all fascinating, just as our trips to the hospital and acting class and karaoke were, Tim. But as usual, I've got to ask. I'm not going to be on a Davis Cup team, so what the heck does this have to do with sales?" Chris knew the connection would be there. It always was.

Tim navigated the final stretch of the journey like a pro. "I'm so glad you asked. There's a tendency in sales to want to close the deal—to get it done—to smack the ball hard. And most salespeople do that with their arm. It's what they've learned. It's the only instrument they know how to use. When going after the ball hard with their arm doesn't work, they get angry and become afraid.

"But if you're going to be really great at sales, you're going to have to build up a set of skills that's more sustainable. Not just your arm, but your entire body. When we went to karaoke, you learned to use your ears and your voice to listen—fully and completely listen—so that you're absorbing not just the words and the notes but also the energy and character of the person you're speaking to as a salesperson. And in acting class, we were focused on developing more awareness of the intention behind things people say and their physical actions. What do people want? How do they express it? Are they pushing you away? Are they bringing you in? Do they need inspiration? Do they need to be lifted up? Do they maybe even need to be put in their place a little bit?

"If you approach sales like Nadal, smashing at that ball every time, sure—you'll 'always be closing,' like they said in *Glengarry Glen Ross*—and that, my friend, is a recipe for burnout and unhappiness. Seriously. That movie, right? But I am here to tell you, you don't have to always be closing. That's not sustainable. There are so many other ways to sell. All these Saturdays we've spent together have been days designed to offer you insight into more balance. More happiness. More sustainability in a sales career. More ways to be in tune with everything and everybody around you, and with yourself, which in turn—believe it or not—leads to more success in sales. The close will come through equilibrium, through awareness, through readiness to respond to subtle cues you're learning to pick up, through moving your body to meet the ball wherever it is. That's what we've been building up your skills to do all this time."

And with that, they arrived at their destination. Chris chewed over the conversation as they joined the excited crowd and settled in for the three-set match. Nadal and Federer were both on fire. Federer, balanced lightly on the balls of his feet, seemed to pivot in any direction in a millisecond, flying across the hard court, returning blazing serves from Nadal. In pin-drop silence, the battle of power versus balance played out before Tim and Chris, and as Federer won the first game, Chris took new note of the ease with which the Swiss player seemed to be dominating the net.

Between the first set and the second, Chris whispered, "So what was up with the hospital and the Bradbury Building?"

"At the hospital and the Bradbury Building, we went inside, and we looked at the scariest place most humans can ever go—our own mind. When we talked about the 'inner corporation,' we established that you are the boss of you, always and forever, and you can structure your supervisory roles in any way that makes sense to you. Your marketing director is selling you at the same time your risk manager is telling you to pull back so you don't drive prospects away. Your other skills—those perceptive skills you're developing through the awareness of voice and tone and intention—they'll tell you which personnel to tap from your inner corporation, and when they're needed. They work together in dynamic tension like Federer's body is working in front of us right now. If you're truly using every part of yourself, there simply isn't enough *time* to rely on just one part of yourself and muscle through. When you fully develop your fear-busting skills—a whole, balanced set of sensory, intellectual, and emotional resources you can use in this career—then you can use them to send the voice of fear and anxiety to its room."

During the second set, Nadal caught a couple of great breaks. His crushing, dominating topspin was respected (and feared) on the pro circuit for a reason, and Federer's ability to get to the ball in time remained human, not superhuman. Tim and Chris applauded every point.

It was a match for the ages. Nadal grew visibly frustrated, unable to make inroads. Federer slowly wore down the younger player. In the third set, though, Nadal took an early lead.

The Swiss master took a deep breath and seemed to grow supernaturally calm. As the rallies grew longer and the pace grew blistering, the balance...shifted.

Federer emerged victorious, 11–9 in the third.

As the two drove back to LA later that evening, the setting sun turned the mountains purple.

"Nadal still has the lead, you know," Chris said. "In overall tournaments, I mean."

"It's not all about winning and losing," Tim answered, shaking his head just a bit. "It's about the efficacy of his approach and about why he'll one day probably be considered the greatest player of all time. It's about his longevity in the game. It's about why he's had so few injuries. And it's about the pleasure he derives from the game. The level of performance he's been able to achieve and sustain is unmatched, if you'll allow me just one little pun."

"Tim, I want to thank you for investing the time and the belief in me. But you know what? I'm never going to be Roger Federer at anything I do! I'll never be that talented. I'll never be that skilled. I'll never be a legend at anything." Chris wasn't down. Chris was completely just-the-facts-ma'am.

"Well, honestly, you're probably right, so I'm not going to argue with you. But you can have the same feeling Roger Federer has. Because I think the moment he collides with that ball and sends it exactly where he wants it to go, he is completely in tune with the universe in his own world. And you can have that in your world."

"I *am* less fearful about sales these days. I don't know precisely which of the things we've done or talked about have helped with that. Maybe it's everything together. But seriously, thank you. In fact, now that I think about it, I haven't heard from Fluffy in weeks," Chris said.

"I am so glad to hear that, Chris. You can achieve that in sales. You probably already have. It's a zone. Everything's clicking," Tim replied. They drove on in silence for a few minutes as sunset turned to dusk.

"Man, that really *was* a great match, wasn't it?" Tim asked. "Everything I could have hoped to see. And more. I hope you saw what I saw out there today—the happiness balance. Two greats, approaching the same job in two different ways. One attacking. One receiving and reflecting. I hope you'll remember today for the rest of your sales career, and not just because Federer won. Although that did make me incredibly happy—I'd have had a hard time convincing you otherwise if Nadal had proved me wrong today and walked away victorious, right?" They both laughed.

"What I want you to always remember is this organic approach to connecting to people leverages every part of yourself. But you must be willing to give up the illusion of control and be present in the moment. Ready to pivot. Ready to move. Ready to change directions. Ready to hear and adapt and change. Not to fear change—to understand that change is the condition of the world and that sales is the process of anticipating those changes. Meeting the ball with your whole body as each moment demands. When you give up what you used to think of as control—maybe those little Rafa-like rituals you do before you start making calls in the morning—you'll become so powerful you actually gain more control. It will come from energy and insight and connection and receptivity to the people you're selling to. All of that is far more important than the product or service you're selling.

"Sales isn't a job. It's a journey of personal development and self-expression."

"So you're saying…I *am* Roger Federer?" said Chris.

"Yes, you are. You're just not as wealthy as he is."

And they drove on into the night.

Tom Talk

In 1968, my father took me to my first live tennis match. We went to see the aging former champion Pancho Gonzales play in the US Open at Forest Hills, New York. At forty, Gonzales was ancient by any professional athletic standard of the day, and as a tennis player of color, he was as stark a contrast to the lily-white audience and his fellow competitors as a fly drowning in a glass of milk. Despite all that, on that sunny autumn afternoon, his greatness soared with each lob that kept him in the point and closer to conquest with every angled winner that hit the corner of the baseline—his perfect precision kicking up an explosion of white chalk like gunpowder accompanying a sniper's bullet. What grabbed me even more than Gonzales's superb play as he shook hands with his vanquished opponent was the glory he now possessed in victory. A seemingly modest man, he received applause effortlessly, waving to the crowd as if we were close friends. In return, our ardent cheering seemed to say, "You are immortal, old man, and by proclaiming our support for you, so are we!"

I have always sought that sense of carrying the day in sales. Whether I was competing against another firm for business, the will of a stubbornly resistant prospect, or just struggling to subjugate my own internal demons, it was the rush of triumph that I craved. The challenge is, the more you give it your all, the deeper the pain when you don't win. It hurts when we strain with all our might and still don't get to the top of the mountain.

When that happens, we must never abandon the belief that the world is an abundant place and always maintain boundless compassion for our own limitations. Emphasizing possibility over futility reduces the amount of stress we create. Kindness as well as passion can help us sustain our enthusiasm and hope. In my view, tennis, in its own way, is civil and forgiving. Despite the exhausting struggle that drives two people to participate in a zero-sum outcome, it's the only competitive sport in which you can have zero points in the game and your total is still called love. —Tom

CHAPTER 10

POSTSCRIPT: ONE YEAR LATER

The silver Tesla pulled up to Canter's Deli at noon. Chris stepped out of the driver's seat carrying a small gift-wrapped box and walked inside.

Tim was already seated and on the phone, so Chris slipped into the booth and grinned, pushing the box across the table wordlessly. Tim picked up the box and shook it, then raised an eyebrow at Chris as he wrapped up the call.

"Guys! You! Oh my God, I can't believe you're back!" The waiter from their first meeting a year prior swooped over with a pot of coffee, two menus, an enormous grin, and the energy of a six-week-old puppy.

"Hi again." Chris offered an extended hand and a big, warm grin. "How have you been? How's acting class been treating you?"

"Amazing news, actually," the waiter said, gesturing with the coffeepot. "I got a series! It's on a streaming service. I can't tell you which one yet technically, but, um, they're famous for selling books? Anyway, it's not just a bit part either. In fact, the shooting starts tomorrow. Today's my last day. I can't believe you guys came in. This must be the universe closing the loop. Do you need a few minutes?"

"I think we do. Wow, congratulations, and I can't wait to see you on TV," Chris said, shaking hands with the waiter again.

"Hey, Morrie," the waiter yelled at one of the guys in the kitchen. "Get these guys anything they want. They knew me when I was *nobody!*" Chris laughed just as Tim was hanging up the phone.

"What in the world is this?" Tim asked, turning the box over in his hands.

"Open it."

Tim obliged. Inside was a signed tennis ball: To Tim, FEAR LESS —Roger Federer.

Tim was, for once, and maybe for the first time Chris had ever known him, stunned into silence.

"How...how...did you...?"

Chris smiled. "I asked."

"You *met* Roger Federer?"

Chris laughed again. "Lord no. I just wrote him a letter. I told him everything you've done for me, from my door-to-door door sales days last year, terrified I was going to end up homeless with my kid, to now. I told him about the match we saw last year. I told him I used to be a Nadal fan—heh—until you showed me the light. And I told him what a huge fan you are. And then I just asked for it. Just like you did when you asked Dr. Edwards Deming about process engineering. I figured, what was the absolute worst thing that could happen? The letter would end up in the trash. So? Nothing to fear."

Tim's eyes sparkled for a second or two with genuine emotion. Holding the tennis ball as if it were a holy relic, he turned it over and over and over in his hands. Then he met Chris's gaze and said, "Well, it looks like the ball's in my court now."

Chris groaned. "You always do know how to ruin a moment, Tim, you know that?"

The two chortled.

"Chris, I can't begin to tell you how immensely proud I am of you," Tim said. "A year ago, you were like a fawn in a forest. You startled and hid from everything. Look at you now. I said you'd be driving a Tesla or parking one, and here you are. That staffing deal you closed with the financial services firm was nothing short of brilliant, and you deserved every single penny of commission on the deal. How's the new house, by the way?"

"My kid still isn't quite used to having a room the size of our old apartment, but she's getting there," Chris answered.

Tim was thoughtful and silent for a few seconds. "I also want to thank you for something else," he said.

"What's that?"

"For arriving back in my life at exactly the right moment."

"How so?"

"Well, as I told you the day we went to that twelve-step meeting, I've mentored other people in sales. But you took to it like an otter takes to water. You never resisted. Anything I asked you to do, you did. You never argued. You never fought me. Any crazy thing I asked, any seemingly insane setting I took you to, any wildly out-of-the-box notion I introduced you to, you accepted. You said yes every time. Thank you for that."

"Thank you for being my teacher, and I know what I must do next," Chris said, smiling. "The student must become the teacher. I must help others on the *Fear Less, Sell More* journey."

And with that, Tim and Chris settled down to the most serious business of the day: deciding what enormous piles of food to order from the star of their future favorite streaming series.

Tom Talk

No journey is ever over. I Googled that phrase just to see if anyone famous had ever said it, but I couldn't find anything. So perhaps I am occasionally capable of a modicum of profundity. At the same time, just about every journey can pause long enough to feel like it's over. In any case, dear reader, Tim, Chris, you, and I have taken a journey together. I hope you picked up some powerful concepts of how you can fear less and sell more along the way. Now it's time to breathe. Hire yourself as the recreational director of your inner corporation. Turn off your mind and relax. Go to a sporting event or an acting class. But whatever you do, don't go back to work. Well, until tomorrow anyway. At which time I expect you to crush it. All the best. —Tom

ACKNOWLEDGMENTS

As someone with ADHD (attention deficit hyperactivity disorder) and dyslexia, digression for me is a way of life. To avoid such folly, I will do something I rarely do and start at the beginning.

By the time I was four, I had accumulated so many problems and challenges that I am convinced to this day that when God made me, he was distracted. So first I must acknowledge all the therapists, social workers, tutors, and compassionate educators who saw something in me that I didn't, believing I could eventually enter normal society—the jury is still out on that.

(I do want to apologize to the Freudian psychiatrist I went to for twelve weeks to cure me of bed-wetting. Not only was I rude and impossibly resistant to her queries, but on more than one occasion, I soiled her couch.)

I'd like to thank the great Wilford Leach for putting me in so many school plays at Sarah Lawrence College. He taught me to make a fool of myself, and in so doing, allowed me to take chances later in life. I want to acknowledge the great acting teacher and president of the National Michael Chekhov Association, Lisa Dalton, for her insights on the art of acting that informed this book. I want to acknowledge Jerry Seinfeld for all the laughs we shared when we started together—not only for inspiring me creatively with his incisive wit and work ethic but also for so outstripping my talent that I left stand-up early, thankfully avoiding my inevitable destiny as lounge entertainment on a Caribbean cruise ship, my career headed for the Bermuda Triangle.

I also want to acknowledge Bob Williams for hiring me as president of film and television at Spotlite Enterprises. I still believe he did it on a dare. I want to thank Howard Tarlow for giving me my start in executive search, a career I have pursued and enjoyed for over thirty years. Thanks to my ex-wife, Lisa, for being there from the inception of SES and taking such good care of our daughters while I was obsessed with running my company and paying the mortgage. To my employees, thank you for enduring my endless chatter and idiosyncrasies, and to my clients, thank you for hiring so many talented people through my company and putting my kids through school. Also, I want to thank my editor, Denise Montgomery. Without her insights, patience, and encouragement, this book might never have happened.

To my close friends (you know who you are), for your loyalty and all the foxholes we've shared. You gave me the strength to keep smiling. To my sister, Peggy, for laughing at all my silly jokes; my brother for playing with me when no one else would; my CEO dad, for modeling professional confidence, and despite my vast capacity for disruption, never downsizing me; and to my mom, for her constant affection and oversized belief in me. A deep, heartfelt thanks to my daughters, Alexandra and Arianna, for teaching me humility as I do the most important job I have ever done, being a father. And finally, to my wife, Susie, who has taught me that joy can come not just from triumph but from comfort and understanding.

 Tom Stern is the black sheep in a family of lions. Tom's father was one of the founders of cable television, and his great-grandfather, a prominent philanthropist, was the CEO and chairman of Sears, Roebuck and Co. at the turn of the twentieth century. As an ADHD child with dyslexia, Tom was unable to live up to those great expectations, and as a result, suffered from extreme anxiety. Over time, he developed a methodology that increased his confidence and enabled him to achieve success in the entertainment industry and founded an executive search firm that has sustained excellence for more than a quarter century. It is Tom's goal to help others achieve success in sales and realize their dreams by overcoming their fears.